THINGS
IN THE
VIKING WORLD

THING Project

www.thingsites.com

www.thingproject.eu

Editor: Olwyn Owen

Maps: Adam Jones Graphic Design

Co-ordinator: Eileen Brooke-Freeman

ISBN: 978-0-9565698-8-2

Shetland Amenity Trust 2012

Cover photo: Collingwood's 'Thingbrekka at Thingvellir', 1897.
             © British Museum (Department of Medieval and Later Antiquities), London.

Printed by
Shetland Litho,
Gremista, Lerwick
Shetland ZE1 0PX

THING
Project **Contents**

'The country shall be built on the law'[1]

The THING Project (Thing sites International Networking Group) was initiated in 2008. Partner organisations from Iceland and Norway took the first steps towards planning the project and established a network with partners from Norway, Iceland, Greenland, the Faroe Islands, Shetland, Orkney, Highland Council in Scotland, and the Isle of Man.

A conference was held in Gulen Municipality, Norway, in June 2008, and a Letter of Intent was signed by representatives of the partner organisations. Plans were made for cooperation on the management of thing sites, improved interpretation and cultural tourism. The application made by all the partners to the Northern Periphery Programme (NPP) also included proposals for the production of educational material, a research agenda and a report on possible steps towards inscribing more thing sites on the UNESCO World Heritage List.

The THING Project is based on the thing sites – that is, the assembly sites spread across northwest Europe as a result of the Viking diaspora and Norse settlements. The aim of the project has been to exchange knowledge, and to develop and test new and improved services for sustainable management and development of tourism at thing sites in the North Atlantic area.

Things were part of an established system for sharing and legislating power, which we can still recognise today. Indeed, some regard these assembly sites as the cradle of democracy in northern Europe. Even today, we can identify many of the old assembly sites by the 'thing', 'ting', 'ding' or 'fing' elements in place names across the Viking world – all of which have their origin in the Old Norse word: *þing*.

THING Project partners and guests at Gulatinget Millennium Park, Norway, 2011.
© THING Project / Frank Bradford

Thankfully, wars and conflicts between countries have decreased in number in recent years, but we are also seeing an increasing number of internal conflicts, civil wars and unrest in countries around the world. At the same time, human rights are under pressure in communities struggling to enhance their liberty. At this time of increasing internationalisation and globalisation, the story of the thing sites is a reminder of the importance of trying to resolve conflicts without resorting to violence and of robust legal systems.

We hope that the THING Project will lead to more attention being paid to thing sites, and increased knowledge about the thing system. But we also believe that the thing sites and their stories have much to teach us today – not least how important it is for societies to be built on democratic values and common understanding.

Thing sites throughout the North Atlantic region offer a wide range of experiences and new insights into the history of democracy. It is our hope that the THING Project will enable a wider audience to appreciate and understand the exciting history of thing sites in the Viking world and the values they represent.

Sogn og Fjordane County Council would like to thank all the partners and participants for their cooperation over the last three years, and for their hard work in carrying out this important project. We hope this is only the start of a lasting international cooperation. On behalf of all the partners, we also take this opportunity to thank the Northern Periphery Programme for their support and interest.

Ingebjørg Erikstad
Director of Cultural Affairs
Sogn og Fjordane County, Norway

Endnotes

1   Quotation from Frostatingslova, the Frastating Code of Law, c.1160-1260.

ICELAND

Thingvellir

◆ Þingnes

FAROE
ISLANDS

Tinganes

SHETLAN

Tingwall

Tingwall

ORKNE

Dingwall

SCOTLAND

◆ Doomster Hill

Tynwald Hill

ISLE OF
MAN

Thingmote ◆

IRELAND

ENGLA

*Figure 1. Map of the western Viking world
showing sites mentioned in Chapter 1.*
© THING Project

*Figure 2. Reconstruction of a Viking
ship at sea.   © Frank Bradford*

Things in the Viking World
Olwyn Owen

At the start of the Viking Age around AD 800, people from the settled areas of Scandinavia began to take to the sea road *(Figure 2)*. The surviving English and Irish sources give the Vikings a uniformly hostile press. 'Never before has such a terror appeared in Britain as we have now suffered from a pagan race, and nor was it thought possible that such an inroad could be made from the sea' wrote the English scholar, Alcuin of York, after the attack on Lindisfarne in AD 793 *(Figure 3)*. The sudden appearance of ferocious foreigners who looked and sounded nothing like anything previously encountered must have been alarming; but one fact above all others united the Vikings' victims in horror against them – they were pagans. These were the 'ravages of heathen men', and the Vikings have left no contemporary testimony to challenge this view. And so it was that their literate and learned Christian victims had the last laugh. It was their epitaph on the Vikings that gave us the heathens and pirates of popular imagination through the ages, their dreadful exploits and heroic deeds of derring-do lamented and extolled in more or less equal measure by writers, historians, artists and film-makers.

But this is only a tiny part of the story of the Vikings. The Vikings might have been alien to the Christian west, but theirs was a civilisation with a vigorous culture and an established system of law and social stratification. The people of Scandinavia shared a common inheritance, a common language, a common art and a common religion – different from those of Christian Europe, but just as valid.

Figure 3. One of the famous ivory chessmen found in Lewis in the Western Isles, Scotland, but probably made in Trondheim, northern Norway. This rook was portrayed as a 'berserker' – a marauding Viking, harking back to earlier times.   *© Davy Cooper*

Over the next 300 and more years, the Scandinavians roamed far to the east, south and west in their magnificent ships – the lords of the seas. Initially they came as raiders and traders, but soon they built links with other civilisations and settled among them. They served as mercenaries at the court of Byzantium and discovered America 500 years before Columbus. They established towns and a network of communications, and exploited the riches of the East. They explored the uncharted waters of the North Atlantic, colonising uninhabited or sparsely populated lands on the margins of Europe. And wherever they went, they took with them a rich array of distinctive facets of their own culture and society – and bequeathed them to succeeding generations of people in what was once the Viking world.

This book explores one aspect of this inheritance – the 'thing' system of law and administration. It focuses on the Viking sea road westwards, from Norway to Iceland,

Figure 4. Thingbrekka at Thingvellir, 1897. A painting by W G Collingwood of the althing gathering at Thingvellir, Iceland. Collingwood had an intimate knowledge of Iceland and the sagas.
© British Museum (Department of Medieval and Later Antiquities), London

the Faroe Islands, Shetland, Orkney, northern Scotland and the Isle of Man. Today, these countries and areas are partners in the EU-funded THING Project. But first, it sets the scene with an overview of the Viking society that gave birth to the thing system and explores some of the issues and mysteries about thing sites in the Scandinavian homelands and further afield *(Figure 1)*.

Things and Viking Society

It may seem surprising, but the Vikings had great respect for the law.

Viking society was highly stratified. We know there was a striking contrast between the wealthy and the poor in society from the huge disparities in the grave goods found in pagan burials across the Viking world, as well as from the evidence of runestones and scanty written sources. Each territorial area had a chieftain or king, supported by an elite class or aristocracy which also provided the fighting force when necessary. Then there was the landowning class of free men, including farmers and merchants. This was a very diverse group, from the king's close retainers and the wealthy owners of major farms to lesser farmers, and formed the largest class in Viking Scandinavia. And finally there were the slaves or thralls.

This pagan society had an indigenous legal system, based around the 'thing' (or 'ting', ON *þing*) which means literally an 'assembly'. Things were a fundamental institution of Viking Age society and were attended by all the free men of a country, province or area. They reflect a remarkable system of administrative divisions of land, which later became judicial districts. There was a hierarchy of things, from local level all the way up to a regional or national assembly (a little like community councils, district councils, regional councils, and finally parliaments today). In this way, local things could be represented at the higher-level thing for a province or land. At a general assembly (or *althing*) all the free men from the thing district would gather to resolve conflicts and legal disputes, whereas only selected people took part at a representative thing meeting. Eventually, the things came to have what we would recognise as judicial, administrative and political functions, as well as a social role. And as always when influential people gather together, the thing was also an occasion for trading goods and sporting competitions, negotiating alliances and cementing friendships, exchanging news, agreeing marriages, and making important decisions with other families and dynasties in the area *(Figure 4)*.

The idea of the thing assembly was not original to the Vikings, but extended across the Germanic world, as described by Tacitus as early as the 1st century:

Figure 5. Bernt Kristiansen's painting of a thing meeting at Gulatinget. He depicts the delegates arriving in Gulen by boat and staying in tents to the right. © *Bernt Kristiansen*

About minor matters the chiefs deliberate, about the more important the whole tribe. Yet even when the final decision rests with the people, the affair is always thoroughly discussed by the chiefs. They assemble, except in the case of a sudden emergency, on certain fixed days, either at new or full moon; for this they consider the most auspicious season for the transaction of business. (Tacitus, *Germania*, chapter 11)

But the Vikings took the thing concept and made it their own, not only in the Scandinavian homelands, but also in the areas they colonised *(Figure 5)*.

The things met at regular intervals, elected representatives, chieftains and kings, made and administered laws, and reached judgements according to the law. The

12th- and 13th-century Icelandic sagas show that legal procedure was complex and precise. Methods of judgement depended on rigorous adherence to a proper code of practice (a law code). In those pre-literate days, the law was preserved by the elders, who observed the practices of the courts and committed to memory the details of past judgements. The law was memorised and recited by the 'law speaker', who also presided over the thing's negotiations, together with the chieftain or king. Decisions were made by casting lots. In theory, 'one man, one vote' was the rule, but in reality, the thing was dominated by the most influential members of the community, normally the heads of clans and wealthy families.

The local ruler may have been military and religious leader, administrator and peacekeeper within the area he controlled, but he was not above the law and many decisions were referred to the thing. All free men had the right to bear weapons and attend the thing. Area things took place at least once a year to settle disputes – about land, trade or debts, for example – make new laws, and pass judgement on crimes such as murder and theft.

The thing system was not really the 'dawn of parliamentary democracy', as some have claimed, though it was representative to a degree. Nor was it an early attempt to be egalitarian and inclusive – these concepts would have been incomprehensible to the men attending a thing, who were well aware of their duties to their overlords. It fell a long way short of modern western democracy, not least in excluding a large swathe of Viking society. But it was an impressive attempt to order and regulate the affairs of a hierarchical pre-Christian society, determining rules for how matters should be managed and settled, and operating justice according to its own world view. Viking society placed great importance on kinship, but the thing system allowed for the possibility that disputes could be settled in a neutral forum and in a non-violent way, rather than necessarily by blood feud. It was a widely accepted and successful system within its own terms, or it would not have been transported to the Viking colonies during this great outpouring of people from the Scandinavian homelands.

Even today, the national parliaments of Iceland, Norway and Denmark have names incorporating 'thing': in Iceland, the *Alþingi* (the 'General Thing'); in Norway, the *Storting* (the 'Great Thing'); and in Denmark, the *Folketing* (the 'People's Thing'). The parliaments of the self-governing territories of Åland, the Faroe Islands, Greenland and the Isle of Man also have thing names – *Lagting* and *Løgting* ('Law Thing'), *Landsting* ('Land Thing') and Tynwald (the Manx 'Thing Field') respectively. Sweden's national parliament today is the *Riksdag* (similar to the German *Reichstag*), but even here the county councils are called *Landsting*, a name used since medieval times for things governing the provinces; and the first levels of the Swedish and Finnish court systems are called *tingsrätt* (the 'court of the thing'). In Scandinavia, there is recognition and justifiable pride that the governance of nations and regions today has its origins in the thing system over a thousand years ago.

Sources of evidence

Documentary evidence: from Viking Age to medieval

The first mention of things in Scandinavia occurs in Rimbert's *Vita Ansgarii* ('Life of Ansgar'). In a famous episode set in the AD 820s, the issue is whether the German missionary, Ansgar, should be allowed to preach Christianity in the Swedish town of Birka *(Figure 6)*. King Björn puts the question to the thing in Birka, but before the thing takes place, he calls his chieftains together and they decide to find out what the pagan gods think by casting lots. At the thing itself, the king's herald then shouted out what was going to be decided – which was that Ansgar could continue his mission. This tale shows that the law and thing sites were also intimately connected with cult and

Figure 6. Some of the 1,100 pagan graves at the Viking town of Birka, where the thing decided Ansgar could continue his Christian mission in the AD 820s.   © Olwyn Owen

religious belief, as we shall explore below. Ansgar's missions to Birka, and then Hedeby in the 850s, were ultimately unsuccessful. It was many decades before Christianity took hold in the Scandinavian homelands.

Unfortunately, this is almost the only written source for things in the Viking period. We lack detailed information about the thing system and its laws, regional variations and the character of thing places before the 12th and 13th centuries. Our main sources are 12th- and 13th-century Icelandic sagas, other medieval documentary evidence (law codes, annals and charters), and place names. It is very important to remember this lack of evidence when thinking about things in the earlier period, and to be cautious when extrapolating backwards in time on the basis of medieval sources.

By medieval times, the dual nature of the thing system becomes clearer in the sources. In essence this is the story of a changing relationship between things and kings. Steinar Imsen captures this well when he writes that there were 'two principles of government in the Norwegian realm in the Middle Ages: one communal and representative, the other domineering and bureaucratic'.

The basic institutions of government in earlier times had been the district and provincial things on the one hand, and the royal retinue or *hirð* (ON *hirð*) on the other. We see this in the episode at Birka in the AD 820s, when the king needs the agreement of the thing to allow Ansgar's mission to continue, but manipulates the situation to achieve his desired outcome. By the 13th century, when contemporary accounts begin to provide more detailed information, generations of kings and their followers, and, later, church dignitaries, had changed the thing system in significant ways. By then, the Scandinavian homelands were unified, each under a single king, and had converted to Christianity. Towns, markets, royal farms and the main churches had taken over many of the diverse activities of the earlier things – public proclamations, discussion and social contacts, engagements and weddings, buying and selling, sporting contests and religious ceremonies – and the medieval things were increasingly concerned only with legal matters.

This increase in royal authority, and its spread into remoter regions, had been built on the success of the king's liegemen, many of them members of the *hirð*, in influencing the traditional assemblies. Many of the *hirð* were powerful magnates themselves, who wielded great influence in the things in their own areas. We gain an insight into this changed relationship from the extraordinary survival of a letter of witness from 1299 (see page 69, *Figure 2*). The lawthingmen of Shetland drew up this document at their midsummer assembly with the aim of clearing the name of Thorvald Thoresson, a royal official and high-ranking member of the Norwegian king's *hirð*. Thorvald was accused of cheating Duke Håkon by a rather brave woman called Ragnhild Simunsdatter. She claimed that Thorvald had embezzled part of the land rents due from Papa Stour. Thorvald evidently felt he had to clear himself of the charges and so, at the next lawthing, he had 'all *logðingismenn* of Shetland' (as they called themselves) write a letter of witness laying out the facts of the case as they saw them and testifying to Ragnhild's intemperate words. The letter was intended to be read by Thorvald's royal lord in Norway, Duke Håkon Magnusson, who was the brother of the Norwegian King Eirik.

Knut Helle has explored what this letter tells us about the political and administrative circumstances in Norway in 1299. Thorvald's title was lord (*herra*), but the *hirð* was mainly a service aristocracy at this time, rather than an accident of birth – comprised of reliable men, often from leading local families, recruited to be royal servants. As a member of the *hirð*, Thorvald enjoyed royal protection and was rewarded for his loyalty and service with an administrative post which gave him a share of the royal income. Thorvald was a ducal sysselman (ON *sýslumaðr*) and represented the king in Shetland. The other important local royal office was held by the lawman (ON *løgmaðr*), who represented the king as the highest judge in the realm. The lawman and sysselman acted in concert, with the sysselman responsible for administration of the judicial system and the lawman for delivering formal judgements at the thing. Sentences were passed under the lawman's instruction, while the sysselman took care of the process and subsequently enforced the decisions. In particular, it was his duty to collect the fines, confiscations and taxes due to his royal lord. The sysselman was more powerful locally than the lawman, with a greater income and a military role, as well as his fiscal and judicial tasks.

Over the next century, the *hirð* aristocracy was gradually transformed into a nobility of birth, as royal control became more embedded across all spheres of public life, including at the things. The ultimate sanction of the things was outlawry – exclusion from the society represented by the assembly. Lesser cases included setting penalties for wrongdoing or determining issues such as land boundaries and compensation. In order to defend themselves against adverse decisions, individuals depended on their own resources and whatever help they could secure from others – if possible, from the most powerful men in the community. In this way, a man could gain protection for his family without losing his freedom, while a lord could gain prestige and influence. The most powerful lords were kings of course, and so the support of the king was the best guarantee of individual rights. Gradually, this delicate balance tipped the scales in favour of the extension of royal authority, which helped lead to the formation of the medieval kingdoms. Another major influence was that of the Church. As

Figure 7. The Norwegian law regions of the 13th century with their main thing sites. The four law regions were founded in the 10th/11th centuries, probably as a result of royal initiative.
© THING Project after Dagfinn Skre

○ Frostating
○ Gulating
○ Borgarting
○ Eidsivating

Sawyer remarks: 'The role of kings as upholders of justice was greatly emphasised by churchmen, who also encouraged kings to act as lawmakers, in the first place in the interest of the clergy and their churches'.

The Norwegian law codes

The creation of the medieval law-provinces was also an important stage in the formation of the Scandinavian kingdoms. Because kings influenced the laws made in regional assemblies, but ruled by consent and had to respect existing rights, they needed the support of powerful men in the community to alter traditional customs and procedures. As a result, the laws in different provinces differed significantly by the time that they were written down between the 12th and 14th centuries.

In Norway, the key source is the laws for the four law regions: Gulating (see Misje, this volume), Frostating, Borgarting and Eidsivating, founded probably by royal initiative during the 10th to 11th centuries *(Figure 7)*. We only have fragments of the earliest Gulating laws from around AD 1000, but a more complete version from about 1250 still exists. The Gulating and Frostating law codes are preserved to different extents in various versions; of the other two, only fragments survive. These regional laws remained in force until the time of Magnus Hakonsson (king from 1263-1280), who introduced a single law for the whole kingdom in 1274 and became known as Magnus 'Lawmender' for obvious reasons.

Figure 8. View of Gulafjordane in the foreground and Sognesjøen, the islands of Solund and the North Sea in the background This typically rugged landscape prompted many Norwegians to take to the sea road westwards.

© Finn Loftesnes

Knut Helle believes the four regions first began to take shape in the coastal lands of western and central Norway in the 10th century *(Figure 8)*. Previously the Gulen thing site had served a smaller area but, in the 930s, Hakon the Good extended its area of authority to all of western Norway and Agder. The combining of earlier thing districts to form a single law region seems the likeliest origin for all four regions, though they emerged at different times. Helle thinks that a change from general assemblies to representative things occurred around the mid 10th century, and was probably modelled on the English legal system developed by Hakon's foster-father, the English King Athelstan.

Within each of the four regions, there would have been a hierarchy of things – things for the *fylki* ('folk'), and for people in specific parts of the area (the *herað* (local), *fjórðungr* (quarter) and possibly the *þriðjung* (third)) – as described in the Gulating Law. The ON word *herað* was originally used to describe a settled district, which could be quite small and usually had well-defined natural boundaries; most, if not all, presumably had their own things. The coastal region was divided into *skeppslag* ('ship-laws') reflecting those districts' obligations to provide ships for expeditions. In truth, we know rather little about the organisation of these different levels of thing. Some commentators think that in practice only the four regional things and the district things actually met. By medieval times, the thing districts had enabled the emergence of systems for raising revenues and increasing the king's resources, including the collection of taxes and the profits of justice – as we saw above in the story of Thorvald of Shetland.

Saga accounts

Several sagas refer to Norwegian thing sites. The first mention of Borg, for instance, thing site of the Borgarting law region in eastern Norway (around the Oslofjord), occurs in Snorri Sturlusson's *Heimskringla, Ólafs saga ins Helga* (*Saint Olaf's Saga*). This says that the Danish King Knut (who was also the English King Canute) held a thing at every *fylki* along the coast and was proclaimed as king, finishing his marathon tour at the thing in Borg, probably in 1028. As ever, we must be cautious about saga accounts. Written some 200 or more years after the events and activities they describe, they may not be reliable – especially when extolling the virtues and achievements of earlier kings, saints and common ancestors.

A case in point is the *Book of the Icelanders*, written by the Icelandic historian Ari the Learned in about 1122. According to Ari, a man called Ulfljot was sent to Norway, probably in the 920s, to adapt the west Norwegian Gulating Law to the newly founded Iceland's circumstances. But the Icelandic *althing* was established around AD 930 –

probably before the Gulating Law came into existence (see Jónsson, this volume). If Ulfljot went to Norway, he was probably seeking clarification of legal matters about which the Icelanders were unsure, rather than bringing back an entire law code. Ari may have had family or political reasons for wishing to exaggerate Norwegian influence on the *althing* over that of the several other lands of origin of Iceland's enterprising immigrants.

The sagas also give us an idea of the layout of some of the major thing sites. In a famous episode, the *Saga of Egill Skallagrimsson* describes the assembly place at Gulating, ostensibly as it was in the 10th century:

> 'Where the court was established there was a level field (*vollr sléttr*), with hazel poles (*heslisteingr*) set down in the field in a ring, and ropes (*snæri*) in a circuit all around. These were called the hallowed bands (*vébond*). Inside the ring sat the judges, twelve out of Firthafylki, twelve out of Sognfylki, and twelve out of Hördafylki'.

The rest of the assembled thingmen stood outside the ring. The Gulating Law itself says the thing site should be circular in shape.

Heimskringla (*Ólafs saga ins Helga*) contains a famous story about Thorgny, a lawman among the Svear at their assembly in Uppsala, which includes a description of the meeting:

> 'On the first day, when the thing was opened, King Olaf sat in his chair and his *hirð* (bodyguard or retinue) around him. On the other side of the thing site sat Earl Rognvald and Thorgny in a chair, and in front of them sat the *hirð* of the earl and the housecarls of Thorgny. Behind the chair and around in a circle stood the peasant congregation'.

After a compelling speech by Thorgny, the people showed their approval by clashing their weapons together to make a loud noise. This custom of making a noise with weapons to signify agreement is attested as late as Magnus Lawmender's time. His law says that a verdict is not legally valid unless the people at the thing assembly give their consent by rattling or raising their weapons in the air (*vápnatak* or *þingtak*).

This same saga also seems to confirm that different laws applied in different districts in the Viking period. In *Ólafs saga ins Helga*, the crafty lawman Emundr, an influential man from Västergötland, meets the king of the Swedes in Uppsala to settle a problem. The problem arises *'er løg vár greinir ok Upsala-løg'* ('when our law differs from Uppsala law'). In other words, Emundr is saying that the law of the Götar differed from the law of the Svear.

The sagas provide plenty of evidence that the legal system did not prevent violence and the wreaking of vengeance. The epic *Njals Saga*, for instance, based in Iceland, deals with a blood feud that spans some 50 years and has dire consequences for most of the main players, despite the escalating disputes repeatedly being taken to thing meetings. Njal himself is burned alive in his house with his wife, Bergthora, and others. The saga concludes with an almighty battle at the *althing*, precipitated by Thorhall, Njal's foster-son, who was trained in the law and was supposed to be advising the prosecutor, but had been kept away from the proceedings by an infected leg. However, when his legal action seems to be failing, an enraged Thorhall lances his boil with his own spear and begins the fighting. After a protracted bloodbath, the priest Snorri separates the parties. The day after, men went to the 'Hill of Laws' where Hall of Side stood up and, with masterly understatement, said: 'Here there have been hard happenings in lawsuits and loss of life at the thing'. Even though his son, Ljot, had been killed in the battle, Hall 'asks those leading the lawsuits to grant atonement on even terms':

> 'In this way the atonement came about, and then hands were shaken on it, and twelve men were to utter the award; and Snorri the priest was the chief man in the award, and others with him. Then the manslaughters were set off the one against the other, and those men who were over and above were paid for in fines. They also made an award in the suit about the burning. Njal was to be atoned for with a triple fine, and Bergthora with two.'

Everyone contributed for the loss of Hall's son, Ljot, which in the end amounted to a quadruple compensation, and the burners were exiled. Common sense and the legal system prevailed, albeit rather late in the day – though even that is not the end of the killing. The story moves abroad and, in another dramatic incident, Kari breaks into the earl's hall in Orkney and kills a man who is giving a slanderous account of those killed at the burning. The sagas are rich in such accounts, interleaving stories of blood feuds and honour killings with attempts to resolve differences between the warring parties at things across the Viking world.

Runic inscriptions

Stefan Brink, an expert on Viking Age law and society, argues that the oldest law-rule in Scandinavia is found on a rune ring from Forsa, Hälsingland, northern Sweden. Probably 9th century in date, this extraordinary artefact regulates the maintenance of a *vi* (a cult and assembly site). Failure to restore the *vi* in a legal way resulted in fines, for example, one ox and two *aura* (*ørar*) for a first offence, rising in severity with repeated offences. The inscription concludes: 'That, the people are entitled to demand, according to the law of the people that was decreed and ratified before' – hence, the law of the

Figure 9. A thing place and one of two runestones at Bällsta, Täby, just north of Stockholm. The inscription says: 'Ulvkel and Arnkel and Gye they made here a thing site (þingstaðr)'. © Gun Bjurberg

land. The ring is associated with *Kungshögen* ('the king's mound'), a large burial mound used as the focus of the thing of the *Hälsingar*.

There are tantalising glimpses of thing sites in the inscriptions of several 11th-century runestones in Sweden, which give contemporary testimony of the existence of things. Two runestones at Bällsta, for example, in Täby parish just north of Stockholm, tell us that: 'Ulvkel and Arnkel and Gye they made here a thing site (*þingstaðr*)' *(Figure 9)*. This assembly location, which included a rectangular area marked out with stones, was created around AD 1010 based on the style of the inscriptions. The thing site was presumably to serve the locality, but the inscription also stakes their claim as leading players in the area.

There is a famous group of runestones around Vallentuna, all connected to a man called Jarlebanke who, by his own account, was very important indeed. One of these (number U212), carved around the middle of the 11th century, tells us that: 'Jarlabanke had this stone raised in memory of himself while alive, and made this thing place, and he alone owned all of this hundred'. A number of thing mounds in Sweden also have associated runestones commemorating prominent people, but do not actually mention the thing.

Place names

Place names are a highly lucrative source of information, not only in the homelands, but also in areas colonised by Scandinavians, such as the British Isles. They are sometimes our only evidence for thing sites, but undoubtedly indicate their presence. Thing-related place names in Scotland, for instance, have led us to Dingwall and several Tingwalls (ON *þing-völlr*, the field of an assembly) in northern Scotland and the Northern Isles (see papers by MacDonald and Gibbon, this volume) *(Figure 10)*. There is a Tinwald in Dumfriesshire, a Thingmount in Cumbria, and of course Tynwald in the Isle of Man – all areas with a significant Norse presence. In Ireland, the Thingmote in Dublin has recently been recognised as a royal inauguration site and meeting place from at least the 12th century. Both Tynwald Hill and the Thingmote appear to have been high status sites with royal associations (see Johnson, this volume).

England, too, contains its share of thing names, both past and present – for historic names can also lead us to thing sites *(Figure 11)*. The name *Thynghowe* appears on a 1609 map at a place where there

Figure 10. Place names in the Northern Isles of Scotland are almost entirely Scandinavian in origin, as on this road sign in Shetland. © THING Project / Eileen Brooke-Freeman

Figure 11. Thing place names in the British Isles. © THING Project

is a distinctively shaped mound, known as Hangar Hill today. This recently discovered thing site, with its associated boundary marker stones, lies on the boundary between the ancient kingdoms of Mercia and Northumberland, now deep within Sherwood Forest. Other English names include two Thingwalls, one in Lancashire and one in the Wirral, as well as a Thingoe (Suffolk) and a Thinghou (Lincolnshire), both probably derived from thing-howe or thing-hill.

Archaeological evidence

The archaeology of thing sites is still in its infancy, with archaeological evidence so far thin on the ground. Structures are not a principal characteristic of thing sites, given that they were not permanent settlements. The physical evidence of a group of people meeting at a place for a few days every now and then is likely to be flimsy – cooking pits and hearths, scant traces of temporary structures such as tents, or the footings of booths (like market stalls) such as those at Thingvellir. Excavations at Þingnes in Iceland, an early thing site mentioned in *Landnámabók* (*The Book of Settlements*), have probably revealed the assembly place, dating from around 900. Recent excavations at Tingaholm in Shetland, however, a definite Norse thing site (see Smith, this volume), failed to locate any evidence of thing-related activities, but recovered disturbed prehistoric material showing that the mound had also been used in prehistoric times.

The Shetland project was carried out as part of The Assembly Project (TAP), which promises further research on the archaeology of thing sites. Landscape archaeology as part of an interdisciplinary approach is likely to be the most fruitful way forward. Examination of topography, place names, the boundaries of administrative districts, old routeways, access to water, proximity to ancient holy or cultic sites, documentary evidence (including historic maps, paintings and engravings), folklore and tradition, can all help to pinpoint likely thing sites.

The nature of thing sites across the Viking world

It is clear that there were differences in thing sites in different areas of the Viking world. It is also clear that assembly sites with a long history changed over time, in terms of their functions, activities and layout.

Thing mounds and hills are a well-known phenomenon of thing sites and were often the focus of the formal activities. Tynwald Hill in the Isle of Man is a striking example, with its artificial flat-topped mound, 25m in diameter at its base and rising to 3.6m high (see page 112, *Figure 6*). At the centre of Thingvellir in Iceland was the *Lögberg* (Law Rock), a hill on the thing site (see page 48, *Figure 6*). Thing sites often also incorporated and reused large burial mounds from an earlier period – as suggested at Maeshowe in Orkney (see page 89, *Figure 9*), where a bank was built around the prehistoric chambered cairn, probably in the Viking period, to define the inner area of what was probably by then a thing place. So thing mounds could be natural features, or reuse large burial mounds from an earlier period, or be specially built mounds, normally with a flat top.

Notable examples in the Scandinavian homelands include the great flat-topped south mound at Jelling in Denmark, built by King Harald Bluetooth in the late 10th century *(Figure 12)*. This artificial mound contained no burial and was part of a planned complex which Else Roesdahl describes as 'superbly designed ... [to combine] visual elements of royal power and legitimacy with structures of religion and law'. She suggests the south mound was a thing mound, built by Harald to serve the whole of Jutland or even the whole kingdom. Jelling was easily accessible, a 'neutral' place with no known important settlement nearby, and surrounded by a palisade defining the physical extent of the thing site. The mound's flat summit would have provided ample space and visual exposure for the leaders of the formal proceedings and their chief men. Pagan and Christian features are represented at Jelling in the form of a huge ship-setting, the impressive (north) burial mound which presumably contained the burial of Harald's father, King Gorm, the Christ picture on Harald's famous runestone and the church – as would be appropriate for a place of royal power at the time of the Danes' conversion to Christianity in about AD 965. The (south) thing mound was erected a few years after the conversion.

In Sweden, examples include Fornsigtuna, the ancient royal seat and predecessor of the town of Sigtuna; and Gamla Uppsala, the royal seat of the Svear, where kings were inaugurated. Gamla Uppsala is known to have been the site of a pagan temple as late as the 11th century, and was later the site of a major church. At the end of a line of massive 5th- to 6th-century burial mounds, there is a flat-topped mound known as *Tingshögen* or *Domarehögen* ('thing mound' or 'court mound'). Recent archaeological work has shown that Tingshögen is a natural mound, but that its summit was deliberately levelled to produce a platform with a stone and clay surface – presumably to accommodate the proceedings of the thing.

Stefan Brink has recently examined some of the Swedish thing mounds, taking an interdisciplinary and landscape-based approach. Another prominent mound called *Tingshögen*, for example, was the focus of the Österrekarne assembly. It lies on a ridge crossed by an ancient road, and was once part of an earlier burial ground. At the foot of the mound is an 11th-century runestone, which was once part of a long row of standing stones on either side of the road. The runestone commemorates a leading local family,

Figure 12. The magnificent monuments at Jelling in Denmark provided King Harald Bluetooth with a physical framework for the exercise of power, religion and law. © Else Roesdahl (photo by Thorkild Balslev)

which was presumably in charge of the thing site. *Tingshögen* is situated next to *Karlåker* ('the field of the karlar') and close to the hamlets of *Viby* and *Ällevi*, both containing the word *vi* ('holy').

The same pattern recurs at the huge mound, *Anundshögen*, part of the earlier burial site at Tuna in Badelunda, with its famous boat-graves. *Anundshögen* was reused as a thing mound and also has an associated runestone, as well as a series of standing stones which lined an ancient road, *Eriksgata*, and led towards a ford or bridge.

So a thing mound, a runestone, and standing stones lining an old road, all seem to have been important elements of Swedish thing sites. A level field was also essential, as we know from saga accounts (the 'level field' at Gulating) and place names (such as Thingvellir, Dingwall and Tynwald), presumably to accommodate the sometimes large number of people in attendance. In Sweden, sometimes the thing name included the element *-åker*, which means 'arable land' and was presumably a flat field. Brink has also noted the frequent presence of a later church and a royal or aristocratic farm at these thing sites. Interestingly, he concludes that although the character of law and legal procedure undoubtedly changed between Viking and medieval times, the physical nature of the thing site showed continuity. People continued to assemble on the same thing site.

A major factor in the development of thing sites was the change from a pagan to a Christian society. Many of the places where major assemblies met were initially pagan cult centres. The place name Viborg, for instance, the most important assembly place in Jutland, Denmark, meant 'the sanctuary in the hills'. The other two important 'lands things' (as they are known) in Denmark were at Ringsted in Sealand and Lund in Skåne (now part of Sweden). Many of these places eventually became significant Christian sites, even the sees of bishops – as at Viborg. The first stone-built church in Ringsted was St Bendt's, founded around 1080. The association of assembly places with both pagan and Christian religion strongly suggests that religious ceremonies were an important component of the activities at thing sites.

Dagfinn Skre has shown this connection at the central-place complex of Skiringssal in Vestfold, Norway, which included the Viking town of Kaupang. Major excavations have taken place here over many years. The urban settlement was surrounded by cemeteries and some 2km to the north was the thing site of *Þjóðalyng (Figure 13)*. Nearby, and north again, was the sacred Lake *Vitrir*, with *Helgefjell* ('holy hill') on its south-eastern shore. Both judicial and cult activities took place at *Þjóðalyng*, and archaeological evidence – cooking pits, post-holes and graves – shows that this was an assembly place from before the Viking period, perhaps even from before AD 600, probably hosting seasonal

Figure 13. View of the assembly place of Þjóðalyng, Skiringssal (1), the aristocratic farm and hall at Huseby (2), the Viking town of Kaupang (3), and one of the Kaupang cemeteries (4). The level of Lake Vettrir, in the foreground, is much reduced since Viking times.   © Dagfinn Skre

feasts. An elaborate church was built at *Þjóðalyng* in the 12th century, the church of the 'moot', showing that *Þjóðalyng* was still a thing site in the 10th and 11th centuries. Men would have assembled here from a wide area, perhaps the whole of Vestfold. The assembly place probably lost its significance after the royal foundation of Tønsberg and its thing site at Haugar around 1100.

Some sites are more enigmatic and fit no pattern, such as Bulverket, in Lake Tingstäde Träsk on Gotland, with its tell-tale name. This comprises a series of wooden platforms standing in shallow water built together to form a square, with sides 170m long. Originally the platforms supported buildings lining an open central square, with the whole surrounded by a palisade of heavy wooden stakes. This site is unique in Scandinavia, but employs similar construction techniques to those used by Slavic peoples of the south and east Baltic areas. It may have functioned as a defended thing site, built by immigrants to Gotland in the Viking age.

The Tynwald mound in the Isle of Man is remarkable for its markedly stepped profile with four levels or tiers (see page 112, *Figure 6*). Interestingly, the Tynwald model may have been replicated at Govan, now part of Glasgow, western Scotland, where Norse influence is denoted by five magnificent Viking hogback tombstones recovered from an early medieval churchyard. The 'Doomster Hill' at Govan, now destroyed, is shown on several early maps, but the best visual record is found in Robert Paul's 1758 *View of the Banks of the Clyde (Figure 14)*. This shows an enormous mound with a distinctly stepped profile, with two clear levels, and surrounded by a large ditch. By far the most likely interpretation of this massive artificial mound is that it was an open-air court site and assembly place. The name of the hill itself refers to the Doomster or Dempster,

Figure 14. Detail from Robert Paul's 1758 View of the Banks of the Clyde , showing the stepped mound known as Doomster Hill.
  © Reproduced with permission of the Mitchell Library, Glasgow

the legal officer who pronounced sentence. Recent excavations strongly suggest that a ceremonial route (radiocarbon dated to the 8th or 9th century) directly linked the early medieval church to the Doomster Hill – just as a ceremonial route links Tynwald Hill to St John's Church. Recent work by Oliver O'Grady has shown that the mound at Tinwald in Dumfriesshire may also have been a stepped mound originally.

Timothy Darvill believes the stepped profile of the Tynwald Hill is ancient and styles these mounds 'the things of power'. The Thingmote in Dublin is also shown as a substantial mound with a stepped profile in a survey of 1682. In short, there appears to be a group of distinctive stepped thing mounds scattered around the Irish Sea area – in Dublin, the Isle of Man, Cumbria, south-west Scotland and Strathclyde.

Turning to the North Atlantic colonies, Alexandra Sanmark has examined the evidence for things in Greenland, one of the farthest flung outposts of the Viking world. Greenland was discovered and named by Eric the Red who built his farm at Brattahlíð at the end of the 10th century in what became known as the Eastern Settlement *(Figure 15)*. The Norse in Greenland thrived for over 300 years, with the remains of some 450 farms identified in the Eastern Settlement alone. There are written references to thing sites

Figure 15. Eric the Red's farm at Brattahlíð, Greenland, was probably also the location of a thing site.   © Edda Lyberth

and thing-related activities at two of the most important farms in Norse Greenland – Brattahlíð and Garðar – and even mention of an *althing* in a letter dated 1389 (though that is all we know of it). Elsewhere in the western Viking world, thing sites were normally located in neutral places, rather than adjacent to major farms. They were often in remote locations, in the middle of or between larger settlement areas with ease of access from a range of directions, in keeping with their judicial and administrative functions, as in the Faroes (see Thorsteinsson, this volume) and even at Jelling. In Greenland, unlike the Viking homelands, there were a very few powerful chieftains at the top of society and a rather homogeneous lower class. Sanmark suggests the Greenlandic Norse chieftains may have been so powerful that they could take charge of the assembly sites more openly and a location close to their farm may not have been as problematic as elsewhere. This is a very different response to that adopted in Iceland, where the *althing* was sited in a dramatic rural location. It was at an Icelandic regional thing in *Þórsnes* that Eric the Red was outlawed for murder in about 980, which led to his setting sail and discovering Greenland.

The papers in this volume explore most other areas of the North Atlantic (Iceland, the Faroe Islands, Shetland and Orkney), as well as northern Scotland and the Isle of Man. They reveal interesting parallels and intriguing distinctions in the nature of the thing sites – close parallels between the Faroe Islands and Shetland for instance, and intriguing distinctions between Shetland and Orkney. Two of the most emblematic and dramatic thing sites, at Thingvellir in Iceland and Tynwald Hill in the Isle of Man, are very different in their physical nature. Dingwall seems to have similarities with Tynwald Hill, but is in a surprising location in terms of the Norse presence in Scotland. But we start in the Scandinavian homelands, with Norway and the Gulating Law – that astonishing reminder of the strong inheritance of things and law-making in the Viking world.

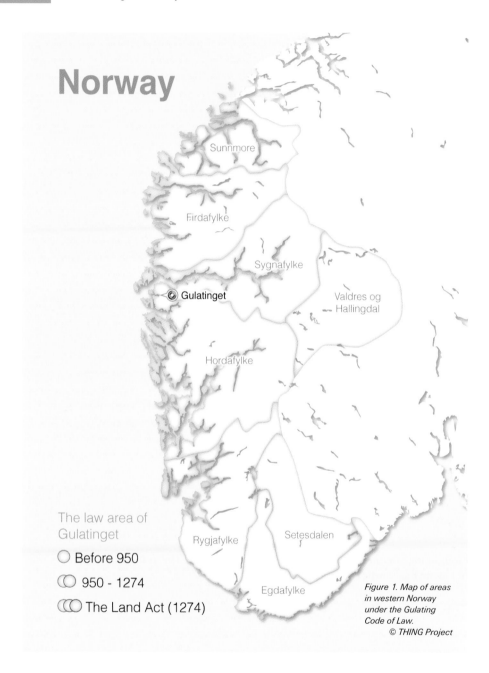

Norway

Sunnmore

Firdafylke

Sygnafylke

Gulatinget

Valdres og
Hallingdal

Hordafylke

The law area of
Gulatinget

○ Before 950

◉ 950 - 1274

◉ The Land Act (1274)

Rygjafylke

Setesdalen

Egdafylke

Figure 1. Map of areas
in western Norway
under the Gulating
Code of Law.
© THING Project

The Gulating Code of Law

Anne-Karin Misje

Gulatinget (The Gulating) was the largest regional ting (pronounced 'thing', meaning parliament/assembly) in medieval Norway. It was located in Gulen, situated on the west coast, between the counties of Sogn, Fjordane and Hordaland, from at least AD 900 until 1300 *(Figure 1)*. The Gulating was a legislative body, a court of law and a political assembly. It started as an *allting*, where 'all free men fit to bear arms' had the right to assemble and participate in the procedures. Free farmers met to deliberate amongst themselves, and later in direct negotiations with the king.

The Representation Principle

By 1274 the regions of Sunnmøre, Rogaland, Agder, Valdres, Hallingdal and Setesdal were added to the Gulating law area. The former *allting* was re-organised into a *lagting*, or superior regional assembly, where each region appointed their representatives. This was the foundation of the principle of representation in the Norwegian system of government.

From Oral Tradition to Written Law

The laws of the region were initially memorised and communicated by word of mouth, until literacy and written culture became established. Men with particular knowledge of the laws (in Iceland called the 'Lawspeaker') memorised and mediated them when the ting assembled. Eventually, around the year 1000, the laws were written down and brought together in a Code of Law – the Gulating Code. This is the oldest known Code of Law in the Nordic countries.

The Rantzau Book

We only have fragments of the earliest Gulating laws from around AD 1000, although a more complete version from about 1250 still exists today. Sadly, the early fragments

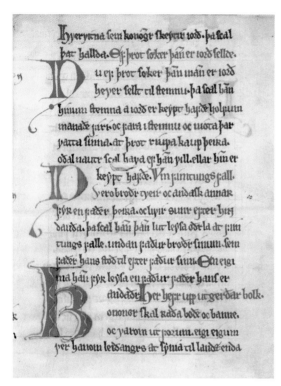

Figure 2. A page from the Rantzau book. This page deals with fees and the military and naval levy known as leidang.
© Royal Library, Copenhagen

and the more complete 1250 law code of Gulating disappeared out of Norway, probably some time during the union with Denmark, and ended up in the private collection of the Rantzau family (hence the name) *(Figure 2)*. In the 1700s however, Christian Rantzau donated the book to the Royal Library of Copenhagen, and here lies Norway's oldest code of law today. This turned out to be a stroke of good luck because the Rantzau library burned down to the ground soon after the donation. We do not know how many other treasures vanished in the fire, but thankfully the Gulating Code survived.

The Origin of the Ting

Although the Gulating reign is usually thought to be from AD 900–1300, it is not certain when the ting and the laws first originated *(Figure 3)*. Both are probably older than the written sources can tell us. We do know that the Code was used as a model for *Ulvjotslova* in Iceland in AD 930, which means it must be older than that. Ulvljot was an observer at the Gulating for three years. He then went back to Iceland, developed a similar code of law to that he had observed at Gulating, and initiated the *althing* in Iceland. Since we know that it takes a long time to develop such a comprehensive code of law, we can assume that the laws themselves are considerably older than can be documented.

Scholars disagree on just how old the Gulating Code may be. A leading Norwegian legal historian, Knut Robberstad, who translated the Code from Old Norse, believes that it must be much older than was first assumed. Historian and expert on medieval Norway, Professor Knut Helle, argues that a ting for such a wide area must have been

Figure 3. One of the two stone crosses in Eivindvik, which framed the original thing site.

© THING Project / Frank Bradford

organised by a king, and could hardly have been established before Harald Fairhair (c AD 870–940) had won control over a greater area *(Figure 4)*. There are also theories that Harald and his son Håkon the Good made the law, and that Håkon established the ting.

But Harald's progress towards gathering Norway into one kingdom ended in AD 872 with the battle in Hafrsfjord, near Stavanger *(Figure 5)*. In the opening lecture of the 4th THING Project partner meeting in Gulen (April 2011), Professor of Law, Ernst Nordtveit, argued that it does not seem likely that Harald and Håkon would have been able to establish a Code of Law in the short time from 870–930. Instead, he claims that it had to be based on a longer tradition, or on imported rules.

Nordtveit asks if it is likely that the Icelandic people, many of whom had fled from Harald Fairhair, would have copied a Code made by the very man who had forced them to leave Norway. Instead, he suggests they may have been seeking to recreate the law that was applied in Norway before they had to leave. He points to the fact

Figure 4. Knut Helle with a replica of one of the stone crosses at Eivindvik.   © THING Project / Frank Bradford

Figure 5. A painting of Harald Fairhair aftter the Hafsrfjord battle in AD 872.   © Knut Bergslien

that the law speaks about 'our laws', and a practice where the citizens had to take care of defence and enforce justice themselves. The Gulating Code of Law is unique in a European context because it guaranteed the farmers a substantial amount of autonomy and self government.

Nordtveit suggests that the ting may have been established earlier than 900, with codes, and that Harald Fairhair and Håkon the Good developed the organisation of the tings further, and made reforms. He points to the fact that the ting before Håkon the Good was an *allting* for all free men, but that Håkon turned it into a representative ting, with a certain number of men from each county (*fylki*).

The Letter of the Law

The Gulating Code contains 320 articles and is divided into 14 main parts (*bolkar*), with a few amendments which are not numbered. It regulates religion (Christianity), contracts (sale and lease of land), ownership (property) and udal right, matrimonial law, inheritance law and criminal law *(Figure 6)*. An important part of the Code concerns coastal defence (*leidang*).

The Gulating legislation is based on casuistic regulation, whereby the law is based on the experience of previous cases, rather than fixed in doctrine. In this way, it develops and acquires further meaning each time that rules are applied to individual cases. Decisions are substantiated by carrying over the arguments used to resolve earlier similar problems and reapplying them in new, but essentially comparable, situations. Over time, this approach leads to the development of more general rules.

Figure 6. Illuminated letter from the Gulating Code of Law chapter on buying. The bride on the right is married by a handshake.   © Royal Library, Copenhagen

The 'Right to a whale'…

One example is G149 of the Code, which regulates the right to retrieve (beached) whales. One of the rules is that the king has the right to half of a whale that drifts ashore, and the owner the other half of the whale – if it is over a certain size. However, it is not clear whether this rule is saying something about general rights to the sea and shores, or if it only regulates the right to the whale. Could it for instance mean that the king owns the shore (as in Denmark)? Nordtveit suggests that it means that the king gets a part of anything of value from the shore obtained by chance by a land owner.

Trade and risk

'If a man buys a horse or other farm beast from another, all risk rests with the purchaser as soon as he has led it away'. This law implies that it is the buyer's responsibility to check the animal for flaws before he seals the deal by leading the animal away from the seller. The law defines the moment of transference of ownership of the animal – as well as the risk of the purchase.

But the law also states the responsibility of the seller. In the sale of livestock, the law lets no one deal dishonestly with another by concealing defects. For example, it is regarded as a latent defect if a cow 'sucks herself'. If the purchaser discovers this flaw during the first month, the seller 'shall take the cow back, or swear that he was not aware of such a latent defect'. Clearly, modern-day regulations designed to protect the consumer have quite a history!

Influence from Other Legal Traditions

A number of theories have been put forward as to the different legal traditions that may have influenced the Gulating Code, but we do not know its precise origins *(Figure 7)*. Legal practices, ideas and principles cross national boundaries and it is likely that they were adopted, imported and exported through migration, together with other cultural influences. The Gulating laws were undoubtedly influenced by several other legal traditions. Canon law was law in Norway from AD 1030–1536 and brought Roman law to Norway. There is also influence from Mosaic Law (the law attributed to Moses in the Book of Deuteronomy) in the Gulating Code. As Nordtveit argued, it used to be thought that a common Germanic law influenced the development of the Gulating Code, but this theory has since been rejected.

Figure 7. Re-enactment at Gulatinget. The lawmen in an historical play (by Johannes Heggland) about Håkon the Good.   © Anne-Karin Misje

Influence from England

There is a strong influence from England through Håkon the Good (c AD 935–961), who was raised by the English King Athelstan as a result of a feud between the king and his father, and who later returned to Norway where he introduced reforms in the way the ting was organised. Later there was substantial contact with England and the British Isles, especially after AD 1030.

One interesting piece of evidence of English influence on the Gulating Code is found in the handwritten document itself. In the beautifully decorated paragraphs of the Rantzau book, some of the enlarged paragraph letters are coloured with green ink (see page 32, *Figure 2*). According to the custodian of the Gulating Code, senior researcher Erik Petersen at the Royal Library of Copenhagen, this indicates contact with England. When visiting the Royal Library in 2008, a delegation from Gulating was shown the Rantzau book. Dr Petersen informed us that handwritten documents from this period in Norway and Scandinavia normally contained blue and red ink, in addition to black, while green ink was normally used in English handwritten documents from the same period.

Another British influence on the Gulating Code is in the laws themselves, especially in the law regarding *Heimsokn*. This law states that it is not allowed to kill a man in his own home and guarantees a man sanctuary in his home. 'My home is my castle' was not just a saying in medieval times and the Viking period – it was protected by law. This may be the earliest evidence of the onset of human rights in Norwegian legislation.

A Sophisticated Legal Tradition

The Gulating Code represents quite a sophisticated legal tradition. For example, the Code makes a distinction between accidents and acts done wilfully, recognising that there is a difference between causing injury or death by accident or intentionally. Professor Nordtveit believes that consideration of the role played by subjective factors when evaluating an act indicates advanced legal reasoning.

The Legacy and Impact of the Gulating Code of Law

The Gulating Code is not a comprehensive codification of all law, claiming to resolve all legal issues, but it is still an extensive body of rules regulating most sides of what seemed important in medieval society and in people's lives. The development of a legal culture, and the idea that conflicts should be solved by law and by independent courts, is a significant break from the traditions of vengeance and bloodshed as the accepted way of dealing with disputes. This medieval legal culture might not meet our standards today, but it is important to remember that the Gulating Code, and the Gulating as an institution, paved the way for our current courts and legal system. The Gulating operated from at least AD 900 until the mid 1300s, which is longer than most modern states have been in existence.

The Gulating Code was an important basis for an act made by Magnus Lagabøte in Bergen in 1274, the *Landslova* (Land Law), which was intended to apply to the country as a whole *(Figure 8)*. This act was formally adopted at the Gulating in 1274, and later at the other major things in Norway (Frostating, Eidsivating and Borgarting). It led to the unifying of Norwegian law across all the things in operation. The Gulating assembly and court continued to meet, but was moved to Bergen at the end of 1200 and lost influence and vanished in the mid 1300s. The court function of the Gulating continued with the Gulating Supreme Court (*Gulating Lagmannsrett*) that still exists in Bergen today. Blood vengeance was abolished during the Gulating reign, and eventually the state took over the punishment of crimes as the Norwegian legal system became more humane.

Remnants of the Gulating Code in Modern Legislation

There is still much influence of the Gulating Code in Magnus Lagabøte's Lands Act of 1274. This was translated into Danish more or less completely in Christian IV's Norwegian Act of 1604. In 1687 Christian VII developed the 'Norwegian Code', which was an attempt to unify Danish and Norwegian law. The influence of the Gulating on the national code of law was by then much reduced, but it still had influence. According to Nordtveit it is fair to say that the Gulating Code remained the primary influence on Norwegian law until 1688 – and so endured for some 900 years.

Norway's current Constitution was introduced in 1814. Parts of Christian VII's Norwegian Code still apply, and there are still examples of rules developed at the Gulating in Norwegian law today. One example is the right of the family to take over a farm that has been in the family for 20 years (*Odelslova*). This law originated during the Gulating period – and still applies despite all attempts to remove it. The Danish King abolished it in 1810, but it was reintroduced in the Constitution of 1814 and given constitutional protection. The same goes for the Right to Access Act that secures a general right for all to hike in the fields, mountains and forests outside of cultivated inland. This principle originated in the Gulating Code of Law and was later codified in the Outdoor Recreation Act of 1957. Likewise the landowners' right to the seabed was removed in Christian VII's Norwegian Act, but this provision never became law in Norway. In short, the Gulating prevailed.

Law texts of this kind will often consider disputed issues or issues that are important to those in power. On the other hand, rules that are self-evident or do not raise any political interest were less likely to be regulated. As a result, we do not know what was uncontroversial in Viking and medieval society. But the laws of a nation give a unique insight into its values and its views on right and wrong.

Figure 8. King Magnus Lagabøte hands over Landslova. Illuminated letter from the Gulating Code of Law.
© Royal Library, Copenhagen

Summary

The Gulating and the Gulating Code of Law, together with the other regional acts, have had an immense impact on Norwegian history. It is a little known fact that Norway has such a long legal tradition. It is important to remember that it takes approximately 400 years to develop a code of law that corresponds with people's values and feelings of right and wrong. It was only because the Gulating was established a thousand years ago that we have a judicial tradition that paved the way for modern Norwegian society. According to Professor Nordtveit, it would not have been possible to establish the modern constitution at Eidsvoll in 1814 without the legal precedent of Gulatinget. In the upcoming anniversary of the Norwegian Constitution in 2014, a primary focus for Gulatinget Millennium Park will be to shed light on the constitutional legacy represented by the Gulating *(Figure 9)*.

Figure 9. Gulatinget Millennium Wall. © Knut Bry

Iceland

Þórsnes ◆

Kjalarnes ◆

⊙ Thingvellir

● Reykjavík

Figure 1. Map of
Iceland and sites
mentioned in the text.
© THING Project

Thingvellir as an Early National Centre   *Torfi Stefán Jónsson*

The history of Thingvellir is not only linked to issues of national governance. Men gathered by the thousands, from all parts of Iceland. Merchants and tradesmen came to conduct business, learned men gathered to exchange views, travellers told news from abroad, chieftains made agreements with each other, men competed in sports, and many others went to seek or offer entertainment in the form of poetry or a good story. For two weeks the Icelanders lived at Thingvellir as if it was a city state.

Establishing a general assembly

Assemblies were set up in Iceland before the country was completely settled by AD 930. *Landnámabók* (*The Book of Settlements*) mentions assemblies at Þórsnes (Snæfellsnes, west Iceland) and Kjalarnes (southwest Iceland), probably founded around 900 *(Figure 1)*. There may also have been other early assemblies not mentioned in historical documents.

The establishment of a single central assembly which would have legal authority for the whole island was an ambitious move, since it would perhaps have seemed more natural to divide the country into smaller districts. There were probably several reasons for this. Firstly, Iceland lacked the inbuilt stability of the settlers' previous societies. The family and clan structure had been disrupted because the settlers came from many different places and families of noble descent had spread around Iceland. In the homelands, families usually sided with each other on important issues, but in Iceland the communities in each quarter or district were not held together by blood ties. The best way to achieve solidarity in the new homeland was therefore an assembly representing the whole country. Secondly, as Iceland was settled by people from different countries with, to some extent, disparate customs and concepts, a single central assembly contributed to the establishment of institutions to tackle the challenge of introducing a single body of law. Finally, overland communications were fairly good in Iceland in comparison to Norway, which made it easier for people to gather at meetings.

After the establishment of the *althing* as the assembly for the whole country, the spring district assemblies became more permanent institutions. They were divided into two sessions, the 'prosecution assembly' and the 'debt assembly', and gathered for four to seven days in May for the settlement of debts and disputes. There were also autumn assemblies, which usually took place when people were returning from the *althing* and lasted for one or two days at the end of July or August *(Figure 2)*. The acts of the *althing* were promulgated and discussed there, but no judicial actions were taken.

From the time of the establishment of the *althing* by AD 930, there had been 36 *goðar* (representatives). This changed in AD 965 when the country was divided more formally into four 'quarters'. Each quarter had three district assemblies, except the North quarter which contained four. In each quarter three *goðar* would hold one district assembly, together with their followers.

Figure 2. Re-enactment of Viking family arriving at Thingvellir for the althing.   © *THING Project / Frank Bradford*

Figure 3. Re-enactment of delegates arriving at Thingvellir in the Viking Age. © *Haukur Snorrason*

There were several ways to acquire *goðorð* (that is, to become a representative or *goði*): it could be inherited, bought or received as a gift. It was also allowed to share one *goðorð*, but only one person could fulfill this role at each assembly, so those sharing the *goðorð* had to reach agreement amongst themselves. Each *goði* was supported by a group of followers from among the farmers. The relationship between *goði* and farmer was based on mutual trust and could be terminated by either party. Each summer, *goðar* had the right to take to the *althing* one of every nine farmers who acknowledged his leadership. Those who were chosen were called *þingmenn* (men of the assembly, singular *þingmaður*) and got paid for their work by the farmers who remained behind in the district. *Goðar* gathered the money and distributed it to those followers who went to Thingvellir *(Figure 3)*.

The *Althing*

The *althing* lasted for roughly two weeks a year. *Goðar* were obliged to meet at Thingvellir and to be there some ten weeks from the beginning of summer, which was around 21 June. At the time of its foundation, all Germanic societies held their assemblies outdoors. This was also the case at the *althing*. Since it only lasted a fortnight, there was no need to expend much effort erecting permanent buildings. The only major development necessary was the diversion of the Öxará (Axe River) through the assembly site in order to provide water for the assembly. The most visible archaeological remains are those of booths dating mostly from the 1700s and 1800s *(Figure 4)*. However, archaeological surveys carried out between 1986 and 1992 and 2000–2006 also located several booths from the 1000s–1300s in the area.

Assembly duties were mainly confined to two places: *Lögberg* (Law Rock) and *Lögrétta* (Law Council). Tasks performed by the Icelandic *althing* were divided between its institutions: a Law Council, five courts and the Lawspeaker.

Announcements of all kinds were made at *Lögberg*, including summonses and anything else that should be made public. People also gave speeches, presented ideas and

Figure 4. Remains of delegates booths at Thingvellir.   © THING Project / Frank Bradford

Figure 5. Thingvellir National Park, showing the Lögberg, Lögretta and Öxará. © THING Project / Frank Bradford

brought up new proposals. The Lawspeaker (*lögsögumaður*) was based at *Lögberg*, where a special space was allocated to him. The Law Council sat on the field in front of *Lögberg*, possibly north or east of the Öxará river *(Figures 5-6)*.

The Law Council was comprised of 39 *goðar*, with an additional nine *goðar* during the general assembly, giving a total of 48, each with two advisors, plus the country's two bishops. So altogether, 146 people attended the Law Council.

The Law Council had two principal tasks, which were to 'frame the law' and to 'make new laws'. 'Framing the law' involved ruling on what law applied when a dispute arose as to the substance of a legal provision (or, as is said in *Grágás*, Iceland's oldest legal codex, when people 'argued on legal questions'). To understand the phrase 'frame the law', it is important to be aware of medieval ideas on the origin and nature of law. These stipulated that the laws pre-existed in human minds and appeared in traditional practices. They were therefore not the creation of any individual, but rather part of the human condition, past and present. Laws were the tried and true inheritance of past generations and were to be respected. Rules were therefore not conceived and adopted consciously and purposefully, but instead brought to light. And as disputes would have been common while the political structure of Iceland was being formulated, the

Figure 6. Lögberg (the Law Rock). © THING Project / Frank Bradford

goðar who sat on the Council's mid-platform were to rule on them in accordance with 'framing the law', thereby revealing the true and traditional law. Older law took precedence over younger. Given this approach, when laws needed improving because they were unclear or contradictory, older and original laws were sought. Behind this lay the idea that laws had been corrupted in the course of human treatment and needed to be corrected.

While it is clear that new rules were in fact often adopted, by approaching the subject in this manner the *goðar* of the Law Council by no means had free rein in their rulings. Instead, they were bound by traditional conventions, recognised interests and the prevailing legal conceptions – in short, the legal traditions of generations.

A majority of the *goðar* determined the outcome, with the minority obliged to abide by this decision, as might be expected given that they believed they were bearing witness to what was considered to be factual. This meant that Icelandic society was not controlled by laws formulated at the will and whim of its rulers; instead, the very nature of the law limited their power.

It was impossible to avoid innovation completely in a society in the throes of shaping its foundations and this was acknowledged with specific instructions on the 'making of new laws'. Although it is not known precisely how new laws were adopted, there can hardly be any question that they required unanimous acceptance. Questions were deemed to be accepted if a good majority of the most powerful and influential leaders gave their agreement, and no one was bound by any decision to which he himself had not agreed. In the minds of people during the Icelandic Commonwealth period, new laws were thus the equivalent of a covenant between free men. The account by the historiographer Ari the Wise (1067–1148) of the adoption of Christianity in the year AD 1000 shows how matters could proceed when a new law was disputed by men of power. On this occasion, one man after another named witnesses, and then both sides – the heathens and the Christians – declared they would no longer share law with the other and departed from *Lögberg*. Society seemed to be on the verge of splitting as people had effectively declared they were no longer bound by the same law. The heathen chieftain *Þorgeir, goði* of the People of Ljósavatn, recommended they seek a compromise:

My advice now is that we refuse to allow those people who are most determined on conflict to decide our course, and seek a compromise between them so that each side gains some of its demands, and all of us have one law and one faith. It will prove true, that if the law is split then peace will also be split.

The power of the Law Council was therefore limited by at least two means. A different arrangement was hardly possible amongst people who lacked a central executive power, as it was necessary to achieve the widest possible consensus. In accordance with these basic ideas, there was also no provision for a national leader. Instead, the Commonwealth was a loosely connected alliance of the country's principal chieftains, and they in turn shared mutual obligations with their followers among the farming class. The governing institutions of the society thus merely performed the function of defining people's rights, not of enforcing them. This has generally been described as a flaw in the constitutional structure of the Commonwealth and as one of the reasons why the Icelanders submitted to the Norwegian monarchy in 1262–64. This may be true enough if seen from a modern perspective, but is scarcely the case if examined according to the premises of the Commonwealth itself. The Commonwealth rejected the centralised executive power represented by the figure of a sovereign ruler.

The Courts

There were five courts at the *althing*, one for each quarter of the country, and a fifth court (*Fimmtardómur*) for the entire country. For a judgement to be passed in a quarter court, 31 out of 36 judges had to agree on the verdict. Failing this, the case was dealt with in the fifth court, where a simple majority was sufficient to decide the outcome. The fifth court was comprised of 48 judges. Each *goði* in the Law Council appointed one judge. In each case, the accused was obliged to remove six judges from the court, and those who were bringing the case, another six. The remaining 36 judges then participated in the handling of the case.

The courts do not appear to have ruled on legal disputes as this was the responsibility of the Law Council. The courts would only have assessed the facts of in each case. The rules of evidence were strictly formal, which meant that the role of the courts was only to judge whether a fact was considered to have been properly established according to form.

The Lawspeaker

The Lawspeaker was chosen by *goðar* and would bear the title for three summers in a row, when they would choose again. The Lawspeaker's (*Lögsögumaður*) chief role was to recite the laws before the Law Council *(Figure 7)*. Originally the laws were unrecorded and this regular recitation of them by the Lawspeaker ensured their preservation. Apart from this, the Lawspeaker directed the assembly proceedings.

In the winter of AD 1117–1118 *(Figure 8)*, a major step was taken when the laws were written down, and additions were made to the laws subsequently. The outcome was the extensive legal codes which have been preserved as *Grágás* in manuscripts from the mid 13th century. Although the text of *Grágás* is generally terse and bears all the characteristics of learned texts, it is the most extensive of all Nordic medieval law codes and indicates the extent of legislative efforts in the new and unformed Icelandic society.

Figure 7. The Lawspeaker directed the assembly proceedings.   © THING Project / Frank Bradford

Figure 8. Winter at Thingvellir. © *THING Project / Frank Bradford*

The End of the Commonwealth

Around 1200 this administrative structure began to disintegrate as a few chieftains acquired more power than others. The first half of the 13th century was characterised by major domestic clashes between the country's most powerful leaders. The kings of Norway had long been of the opinion that countries which had been chiefly settled from Norway were in one way or another subject to their sovereignty. By the mid 13th century, royal power in Norway had grown considerably in strength. After severe fighting and bloodshed amongst the main chieftains, the Norwegian king's control over Iceland was signed and sealed in 1262–64, when all the country's principal leaders swore their loyalty to him and agreed a special covenant laying down both parties' rights and obligations. The Icelanders agreed to pay the king a certain sum in tax, but reserved the right to be involved in the setting of laws. In return, the king promised to ensure peace in Iceland, together with certain other specific rights, such as six merchant ships would come to Iceland every year to deliver goods. For the Icelandic chieftains this was a good solution. The king was a long way away and had scant means of exercising his power in Iceland, and so the chieftains retained their power albeit now in the king's name. But from the time of this contract onwards, the members of the Law

Council were no longer *goðar* with a special relationship with their follower farmers: instead, the king appointed men to the Law Council. Thingvellir continued as the place of assembly for many more generations of Icelanders, but its days as the national centre of an independent Iceland were over *(Figure 9)*.

*Figure 9. Today Thingvellir is "a protected
national shrine for all Icelanders".
© Einar Á.E.Sæmundsen*

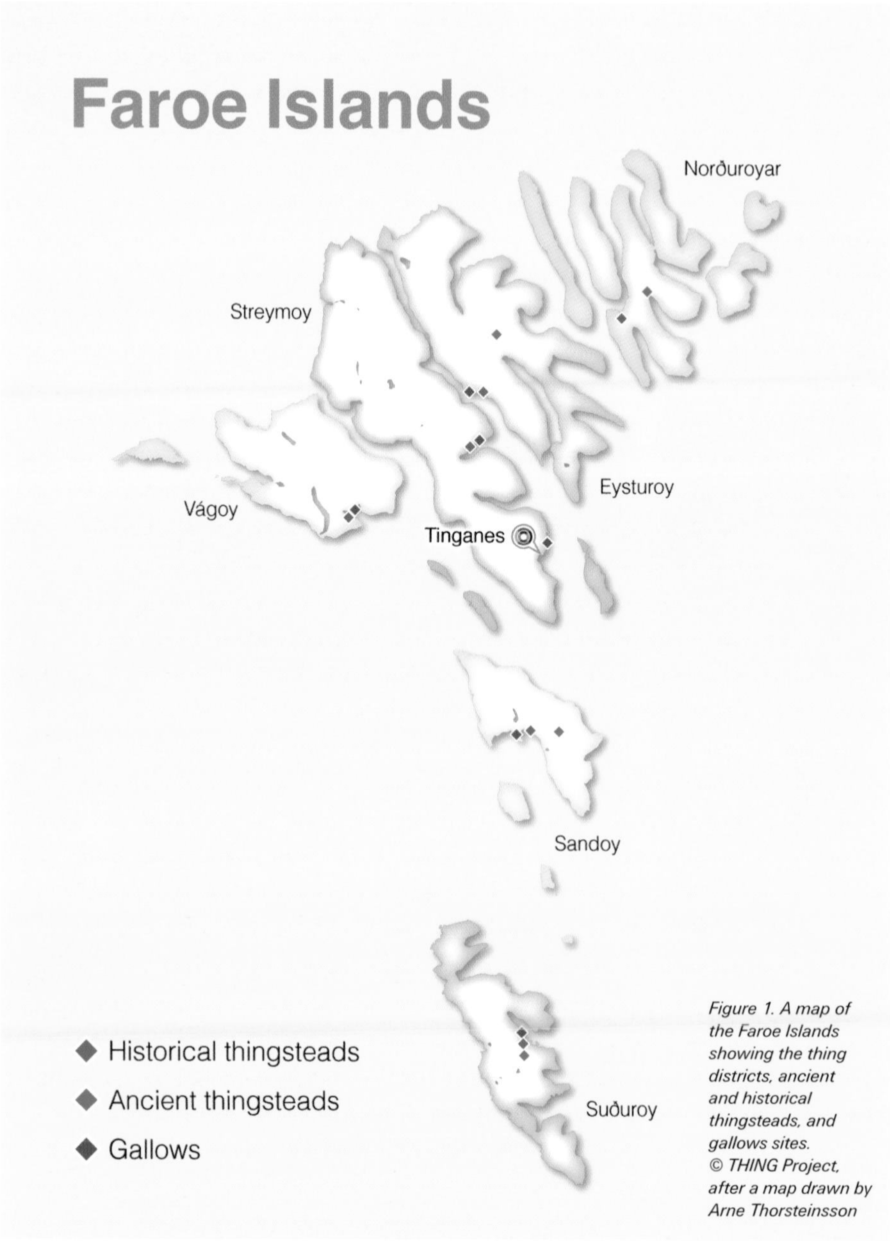

Faroe Islands

Norðuroyar

Streymoy

Vágoy

Eysturoy

Tinganes

Sandoy

◆ Historical thingsteads

◆ Ancient thingsteads

◆ Gallows

Suðuroy

Figure 1. A map of the Faroe Islands showing the thing districts, ancient and historical thingsteads, and gallows sites.
© THING Project, after a map drawn by Arne Thorsteinsson

District Thingsteads in the Faroe Islands   *Arne Thorsteinsson*

The Thing System

The main thing in the Faroe Islands was held in Tórshavn at high summer. This was the *alting* until the second half of the 1270s, but later became a *løgting* (lawthing). District things were held around the country in the spring, though there are some references to autumn things, too. Some Faroese place names have *ting* or *dóm* (meaning 'thing' or 'verdict') incorporated into the name, as in Tinghellan and Dómheyggjar, indicating that meetings were held at these places, although they were not proper thingsteads.

From as far back as we know, the Faroe Islands were divided into six thing districts: Suðuroy, Sandoy, Vágoy, Streymoy, Eysturoy and Norðuroyar *(Figure 1)*. The district things were lower courts than the *alting* (or lawting) in Tórshavn, and cases at a district thing could be transferred to the main thing if necessary. Nonetheless, the district things had the power to impose and carry out serious sentences, including corporal punishment and death sentences, and places of execution formed a part of most district thingsteads.

The oldest preserved court book dates from 1615, before which little is known about the activities of district things. The district things dealt with both civil and criminal cases, and official announcements might also be made there. The court consisted of the *løgmaður* (the chief justice) if he was present, and six *goðar* (representatives) from the district who had been appointed by the *fútin* (the bailiff), who acted as prosecutor when he was there. Otherwise, the *sýslumaður* (the local sheriff) would be responsible for the prosecution. The same six men also represented the district at the *løgting*, which thus had 36 members, six from each district. The *sorenskrivari* (the sworn secretary) recorded proceedings in the court book at all the district things, as well as at the *løgting*.

The limited surviving written sources show that district things were held indoors in certain villages. However, there are oral traditions of sites where things are thought to have been held in ancient times, often located far away in the outfields.

This paper considers things and thingsteads by district – dealing firstly with the thingsteads recorded historically, then those known from oral tradition, and lastly, the associated places of execution.

Suðuroy

The Suðuroy thing district comprised the whole island of Suðuroy. In historical times the thing was held in the village of Ørðavík in the centre of the island (Figure 2).

Oral tradition has it that the ancient thingstead was located in the mountains above the village, on the path ascending towards Fámjinsskarð and close to the main route on the island, between Mannaskarð to the south and Oyrnaskarð to the north. The actual place is called uppi millum Stovur. Members of the thing are said to have erected their tents at Tjaldavík, which lies immediately south of Ørðavík, though it is a fair walk from here to the thingstead itself.

Towards the end of the northern shore of Ørðavík bay, between the bay and Trongisvág, is Gálgin, a name which means the gallows. There are other related names in the area, such as Gálgatangi and Gálgagjógv, literally Gallows Point and Gallows Gorge. One tradition has it that thieves were hanged from a wooden plank placed across Gálgagjógv, but this seems unlikely: it may have originated as no more than an explanatory tale for an intriguing place name.

Figure 2. The village of Ørðavík seen from the road that goes up past the ancient thingstead uppi millum Stovur. To the right we see Tjaldavík, with the islet of Tjaldavíkshólmur. The village of Froðba can be seen in the background. To the left we see Gálgin, between the bays of Øðravík and Trongisvágur. © Arne Thorsteinsson

Although we have only place names and folk stories to guide us, it is likely that the gallows was sited high up on the headland between Ørðavík and Trongisvág. This site would have given an unrestricted view of the gallows from three villages: Ørðavík, Trongisvágur and Froðba. Unfortunately, we do not know for sure as no death sentence was carried out in Suðuroy after 1615, the date of the oldest preserved court book.

Sandoy

The Sandoy district covered the islands of Skúvoy and Dímun, as well as the main island of Sandoy. The historical thingstead was on the farm í Trøðum in the village Heima á Sandi. In the infield, a short distance from the farmstead, there is a stone which bears the name Tingborðið, meaning the thing table *(Figure 3)*. The date 1789 is carved on the stone, together with the letters 'RL'.

Figure 3. Tingborðið (the thing table) on the farm í Trøðum on Sandoy.   © THING Project / Frank Bradford

The ancient thingstead is said to have been at millum Vatna, meaning the area between the two small lakes, at a point some distance east of the village Heima á Sandi, and more or less equidistant from the villages of Heima á Sandi, Skálavík, Húsavík and Skarvanes.

Uppi á Gálga is the name of a spot úti í Nesi, west of the infield of Heima á Sandi, above the settlement í Horni and close to the edge of the cliff to the west. Today a cairn occupies this conspicuous place, which can be seen from all directions, including from

Figure 4. Á Gálga on Sandoy. The gallows stood where the cairn stands now.   © Símun V. Arge

all parts of the village Heima á Sandi and from Skarvanes *(Figure 4)*. Legend has it that if a condemned person could climb to the top of the gallows three times in a row, then they would be freed. One story tells of a man nicknamed Runti who was condemned to be hanged in the mid 17th century for the theft of a cow. He managed to get to the top of the gallows twice, but on his third attempt the priest got a bystander to distract him so that he failed. Runti was hanged, but the fish disappeared from the waters surrounding Sandoy for the next three years, which was seen as punishment for Runti's unjust execution.

This story probably originates in the death sentence of Hans Esaiasson for theft. Hans was first convicted of theft in 1626, when he was fined four guilders for having stolen a ewe from the priest in Sandoy. At the Sandoy district thing in 1638, he again pleaded guilty to theft. This time he had stolen five sheep carcasses, some cheese and some other food items in Skarvanes. Later he was accused of stealing two sheep carcasses, and another two sheep carcasses on another occasion, again from the priest. There are no records of how Hans was executed, but thieves were usually hanged.

Vágoy

The island of Mykines was part of Vága thing district. The historical thingstead was situated á Ryggi in the village of Miðvágur, but there is no reliable information about an ancient thingstead in Vágoy.

At Giljanes, on the border between the villages of Miðvág and Sandavág, there is a place called inni á Gálga and a boulder named Gálgasteinur. The gallows may have stood at this place, but nobody was hanged here after 1615.

Streymoy

Streymoy was probably the most populous thing district in the country and included the islands of Nólsoy, Hestur and Koltur. The historical thingstead was located in the settlement called við Sjógv in the village of Kollafjørður, where one of the houses is called í Tinggarðinum (thing farm) *(Figure 5)*. A short distance away from the settlement is a place called Gálgin (the gallows), and stories are told about a place where the condemned could save themselves if they managed to reach it. Again, nobody has been hanged in Kollafjørður since 1615.

There is no mention of an ancient thingstead in Streymoy thing district, apart from the main thing at Tinganes in Tórshavn, of course.

Figure 5. í Tinggarðinum in the village of Kollafjørður, Streymoy.
© THING Project / Frank Bradford

Figure 6. Ancient thingstead in Eysturoy is located at Stevnuválur.   © *THING Project / Frank Bradford*

Eysturoy

The thing district of Eysturoy comprised only the island of Eysturoy. The historical thingstead was in the village of Selatrað. Tradition points to a large stone called Tingsteinur, although the thing at Selatrað was probably held indoors.

Down by the shore there is a place called á Gálga, where a thief was hanged in 1626 *(Figure 10)*. The thief, Pætur Jákupsson, had been stealing habitually over a long period and from many places. He admitted to having stolen fish, mutton, whale meat, blubber, cheese and other food, as well as trousers, socks, shoes and sheep skins, at various places in Eysturoy, Streymoy and Vágoy. He was condemned to be hanged. That same year, Jákup á Toftum, who may have been Pætur's father, was sentenced to pay a fine of one mark because he did not turn up at the Seletrað thing to escort Pætur to the gallows.

The ancient thingstead in Eysturoy is thought to have been at Stevnuválur *(Figures 6 and 11)*. This is located in the middle of the area between the firths of Skálafjørður and Funningsfjørður, quite some distance from Selatrað.

Norðuroyar – the Northern Islands

The main island in this thing district is Borðoy, where the thingstead used to be. To the west is Kalsoy and Kunoy, and to the east Viðoy, Svínoy and Fugloy. The historical thingstead was in the settlement called í Vági, in the village *inni í Bø*, which later developed into the town of Klaksvík.

The ancient thingstead of Norðuroyar, named í Køtlum, was situated in the mountains north of Klaksvík, straight up from the village í Árnafirði, and by the path that goes north around the hill past Áarskarð *(Figure 7)*. It lies as near to the centre of the thing district as possible. A large boulder called Tingsteinur stands here, with smaller stones erected around it, but it is not known when this stone setting was built.

There is no known reference to a place of execution in Norðuroyar, yet we know that people were hanged here. In 1657 Niels Antoniussen was found guilty of theft at the district thing í Vági, which had happened thrice before. He had been flogged, and the last time he was taken to the thing í Vági, he was warned that if he stole again he would be executed. Undeterred, in 1657 Niels stole eight sheep carcasses, two pairs of socks, some tallow and two skins – and this time there was no mercy. Niels Antoniussen was to be sent to the gallows, unless the bailiff decided to pardon him on behalf of the king. There is no indication that the bailiff chose this option and it is

Figure 7. The ancient thingstead í Køtlum in Norðuroyar.   © *Robert Joensen. Norðoya Fornminnissavn*

almost certain that Niels was hanged í Vági. However, in the absence of any place name evidence or oral tradition, we do not know where the gallows was sited.

According to one oral account, in ancient times there used to be a thing at Selheyggur, close to the farm í Vági. One story has it that, if someone was condemned to death, they could save their life if they ran all the way from Selheyggur up to Hálgafelli without being caught, and then fell to their knees before the altar there. It is unlikely there was ever a thing at Selheyggur but, if there is any truth in this story, this may possibly have been the site of the gallows.

The Main Thing in Tórshavn

As far as we know, the Faroese *alting*, later the Faroese *løgting*, has always been held on the Tinganes headland in Tórshavn *(Figure 8)*. Since at least the beginning of the 16th century, the Thing has been held in the building *Tingstovan*, near the outer end of the headland. Before *Tingstovan* was built, the Thing is said to have been held outdoors.

A little further towards the mainland lies Saðlingarhella. According to oral tradition, if a condemned person could flee to this place they were saved. In all likelihood this is another explanatory tale for the place name, which people have connected to the word *sælur*, meaning 'saved'.

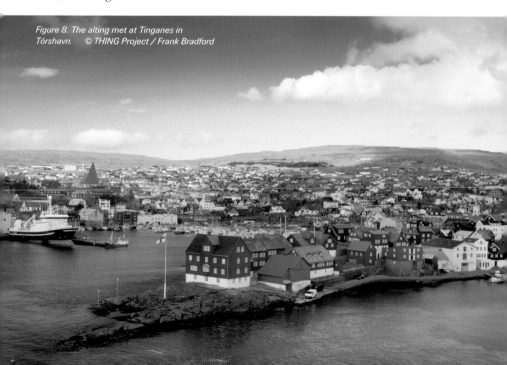

Figure 8. The alting met at Tinganes in Tórshavn.   © THING Project / Frank Bradford

There are three places of public punishment in Tórshavn: the place where the gallows stood; a place for flogging; and a place where offenders may have been beheaded and the head raised upon a spike.

On the east side of the present town, there is a place called á Gálga, and references to a couple of stones named Gálgasteinar, both names obviously derived from the gallows (Figure 9). It can be assumed the gallows was placed so that it was

Figure 9. The path to Gálgasteinar on the hill east of Tórshavn.
© THING Project / Frank Bradford

visible not only from Nólsoy and Hoyvík, but also from Argir and from Tórshavn itself, but further study is needed to determine the exact site.

On the east side of the bay, there is a place called á Kák, which is where lawbreakers were *kákstrokin*, or flogged. This was the punishment for thieves and other wrongdoers if the transgression was not serious enough for the death sentence.

Beneath Skansin, the old fortress, there used to be a spit of land, which now lies under the pier, called *Steglingartangi* (*stegla* = spike), and later *Stangarnes* (*stong* = pole). Two coffins are said to have been found in the vicinity and it seems quite probable that this was the place where condemned people were beheaded. The head, and perhaps the body too, would have been impaled on a spike – a theory supported by legal documents.

From some time between 1564–83 and till 1688, sexual offences were dealt with according to the Icelandic law, *Stóridómur*. Serious offences of this kind might be punished by flogging, while incest was punished by death. Men were beheaded and women were drowned in the bay. According to *Stóridómur*, verdicts which could result in corporal punishment or execution seem only to have been passed at the *løgthing*.

Conclusions

It will be clear from this short outline that there is considerable scope for further research on thingsteads in the Faroe Islands. This should include studies of place names, oral traditions and documentary evidence, as well as topographical surveys of all the known and possible thingsteads in their landscape context. Meanwhile, some tentative conclusions may be drawn.

Figure 10. Á Gálga at the shore at Selatrað in Eysturoy.   © *THING Project / Frank Bradford*

In four of the thing districts, the references to ancient thingsteads suggest they were all located away from the settlements, but near important routes between the villages. In Suðuroy and Norðuroyar the thingsteads were located high in the mountains, whereas in Sandoy and Eysturoy they were on lowland sites. In the same way as the main thing in Tórshavn is situated in the middle of the Faroes, these thingsteads were located centrally within their thing district to give the easiest possible access from the villages in the district.

When thingsteads were moved into settlements, they were almost always relocated to the nearest settlement. Eysturoy is the exception to this rule. Here, the thingstead was moved all the way to Selatrað on the west side of the island, which weakened its physical connection to most other settlements in the thing district.

In Vágoy and Streymoy, the references to an ancient thingstead are few and vague. Unfortunately, it may not be possible to locate these sites, other than perhaps through place name research.

Names which allude to gallows are found in five of the six thing districts, and in all cases these names are found near to the sites of known historic thingsteads. This can be seen most clearly in Eysturoy, where a *gálga* name exists in Selatrað *(Figure 10)*, but no such name has been found in connection to the thingstead at Stevnuválur. It is therefore not possible to use the local *gálga* names in Vágoy or Streymoy to determine where the ancient thingstead was located. This, and the fact that many of the gallows have not been used since 1615, tells us that the relocation of the thingsteads, from uninhabited places to within settlements, happened before 1615 – perhaps a long time before.

The gallows seem in most cases to have been placed on high ground where they were clearly visible, so that as many people as possible could see with their own eyes what befell those who committed serious offences. It is difficult, though, to pinpoint the exact sites of the gallows, because names like *gálgasteinur* and *gálgagjógv* are derivatives and the name *á Gálga* is never precisely located.

It is perhaps surprising that no whipping posts have been found outside Tórshavn, since flogging was just as much a part of the legal system as the death penalty.

Likewise, it is probable that spikes or poles were normally placed in the vicinity of the district things as part of the furniture of punishment.

It is interesting to note that there are several examples – from Sandoy, Kollafjørður, Klaksvík, Tórshavn, and other places too – of the belief that a condemned individual had a chance to save themselves by performing a certain feat. This does not fall directly under the definition of the concept of *judicium Dei* (where judgements determined by trials or ordeals are seen as judgements of God), but the popular belief that a condemned person could save their life by achieving some feat or surviving an ordeal is related to this idea. *Judicium Dei* was legally part of the production of evidence and was a common belief in ancient and medieval times. In reality, it was almost always impossible for a person sentenced to death to avoid execution by performing a feat, but it meant that God (or the gods) would pass final sentence and, in theory at least, this could contradict the sentence meted out by people. The clearest manifestation of God's sentence in the Faroes is the story of Runti, where God apparently punishes the people of Sandoy for Runti's unjust killing. In 1215 the papacy banned Christians from using *judicium Dei* in court cases, but this belief seems to have lived on among the people.

The church authorities reintroduced *judicium Dei* in the late Middle Ages and, after the Reformation in Scandinavia, it famously became an accepted part of the witch hunt, although this never had much influence in the Faroes.

There is much still to discover about thingsteads in the Faroe Islands and the legislative system underpinning activities at the district things. In particular, it should be noted that specific research into Faroese law in relation to the thingsteads has yet to be undertaken – and could be an important factor in understanding the origins of the Faroese judicial system today.

*Figure 11. Stevnuválur, millum Fjara,
in Eysturoy.
© THING Project / Frank Bradford*

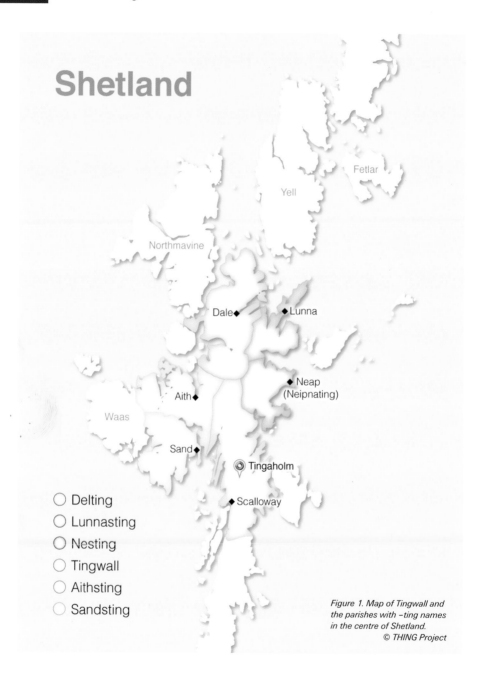

Figure 1. Map of Tingwall and
the parishes with –ting names
in the centre of Shetland.
© THING Project

Shetland's Tings

Brian Smith

If we want to understand Shetland's assembly sites – our 'tings', as we call them – we must start by reconsidering any assumptions we may have that they were always parliaments of free men. During the period when we have records, from 1299 onwards, Shetland's tings were dominated by representatives of the crown, to a greater or lesser extent.

Prior to King Magnus's reign (1263-80) Shetland may have had an *althing*, an assembly of free men. It is difficult to believe that the impressive site at Tingwall first came into use as late as the 13th century. Right in the centre of the islands, next to the head church and archdeacon's house, it looks ancient *(Figure 1)*.

King Magnus and his successors were exerting more and more control in their provinces – even in Iceland. There, and in the Faroes and Shetland, the assemblies stopped making their own laws, if that is what they had been doing, and became places where royal legislation was promulgated and enforced. They became *lawtings*.

We know what was happening in Shetland around 1300 because we have place names – for instance, Tingaholm, the name of our *lawting* site. We also have documents. Shetland's oldest surviving record, written by the

Figure 2. Shetland's oldest surviving record, written by the lawman of Shetland in 1299.   © Arnamagnæan Institute, Copenhagen

lawman of Shetland in 1299, records a decision that the lawthingmen of Shetland had made *(Figure 2)*. Archaeology can tell us little about assemblies and how they worked. From the names and the documents, however, we can learn not only where the participants gathered, but who they were and what they were doing.

In recent years the Norwegian historian Steinar Imsen has thrown much light on the officials who met at Tingwall, and what they were up to. Wielding King Magnus's lawcode, they represented the crown, and were sometimes Norwegians themselves. But they interacted with the local community too. The Shetlanders could negotiate with the officials, and the documents show us how they did so; but the officials were firmly in charge.

We know from documents, and from local tradition, that the officials carried out their deliberations almost surrounded by water at the loch of Tingwall: on Tingaholm. Prior to the 1850s the tingstead was a holm in the loch, linked to the mainland by a stone causeway *(Figure 3)*.

John Brand, visiting Shetland in 1701, reported that 'three or four great Stones are to be seen, upon which the Judge, Clerk and other Officers of the Court did sit'. Meanwhile, the other participants 'sat in the open field' below the kirk.

Figure 3. Painting of the tingstead linked to the mainland by a stone causeway, by Thomas Woore, 1828.
Courtesy of Mrs Prudence Heath

'All the Country concerned to be [at Tingwall]', Brand went on, 'stood at some distance from the Holm on the side of the Loch, and when any of their Causes was to be Judged or Determined, or the judge found it necessary that any Person should compear before him, he was called upon by the Officer, and went in by these steping stones, who when heard, returned the same way he came'. Of course, there must have been times when bad weather made shelter imperative. In May 1307, for instance, the officials made their decision in the archdeacon's kirk next door *(Figure 4)*.

Brand heard an interesting story about the *lawting's* proceedings. His informants told him 'that when any Person received Sentence of Death upon the Holm, if afterwards he could make his escape through the crowd of People standing on the side of the Loch, without being apprehended, and touch the Steeple of the Church of Tingwal, the sentence of death was Retrieved, and the Condemned obtained an Indemnity: For this Steeple in these days was held as an Asyl for Malefactours, Debitors Charged by their Creditors &c. to flee into.' Sanctuary in churches was common in medieval Europe.

Figure 4. Tingwall Kirk with the remains of the earlier kirk on the left. © Davy Cooper

Steinar Imsen has also suggested that, after the Black Death, which came to Shetland in 1349, the part played in the proceedings by native Shetlanders may have increased. Far away from Copenhagen, and eventually from Edinburgh, the Shetlanders may well have had more autonomy in those poverty-stricken times. We have a reference to a letter announcing the election of one of them, Nicol of Aith, as 'lawman generale of all Yetland', by his peers, dated at the 'ting holm' of Tingwall in July 1532, and authenticated by the common seal of the islands. But there was always tension at the *lawting* between royal and local representatives. And it seems to have been partly resolved in the crown's favour in the late 1540s, when the last Shetland lawman left office.

There were no more lawman appointments, and the Shetlanders were displeased. In 1577 more than 750 of them came to Tingwall to complain about Lawrence Bruce, a tyrannical official.

They were at pains to explain what they thought their *lawting* should be. 'This lawting', they told the visitors, 'is the principall court haldin in the cuntrie in the haill yeir, to the quhilk all men aucht to cum … that hes land and heritage or grit takkis [leases] of the king' ('is the principal court held in the country during the year, to which all men ought to come … who own land and heritage, or hold big leases from the king'). They believed that they themselves should organise the proceedings: 'Na men', they said, should deliberate on cases 'bot cuntriemen that kennis thair awin lawis' ('except countrymen who know their own laws').

More than a quarter of a millennium after the formation of the *lawting*, the Shetlanders were still fighting to have their say there.

In the early 1570s Lord Robert Stewart had moved the *lawting* from Tingwall to Scalloway. No doubt Robert had a house there, and it must have seemed that the royal officer was taking the institution into his own hands. The *lawting* remained at Scalloway, and was eventually held in the great hall of Earl Patrick Stewart's new castle in the village *(Figure 5)*. In August 1604, for instance, 'the lating court of the contrie of Yeitland, callit the principall and heid court thairof' ('the lawting court of the country of Yetland, called the principal and head court thereof') was presided over

there by Patrick himself. More than half the jurors were Shetlanders, small landowners: things had improved slightly since the 1570s. And they were still consulting 'the chepturis of the law buik' ('the chapters of the lawbook'), Magnus Lawmender's lawcode of the 1270s, in their proceedings.

But the *lawting's* days were coming to a close. The last reference we have to it is from 1608. Earl Patrick fell from power soon afterwards. After a short period of chaos, the crown swept away Shetland's laws and local institutions in 1611. Shetland's *lawting* became a sheriff court. The holm at Tingwall, disused since the 1570s, gradually became a historic monument *(Figure 6)*.

Figure 5. Earl Patrick Stewart's castle in Scalloway, built in 1599. © Davy Cooper

Figure 6. Tingaholm as it is today.   © *THING Project / Frank Bradford*

But that's only one-third of the story of Shetland's tings. There are half-a-dozen place names in Shetland with '-ting' in the second part of them. This is a very unusual situation. Such names are uncommon anywhere; to have so many in Shetland requires explanation.

They are the names of parishes, which form a sort of circle in the centre of the islands: Delting, Lunnasting, Nesting, Sandsting and Aithsting, with Tingwall to their south *(Figure 1)*. There must have been a ting in each place. With the exception of Nesting, the -tings are named after townships: Dale in Delting *(Figure 7)*, Lunna in Lunnasting, Sand in Sandsting and Aith in Aithsting. Some of these places were the sites of parish churches: that is, they were important places. They may have been the homes of local potentates as well.

Gillian Fellows-Jensen believes that Shetland's -ting names are late, and I agree with her. But what is their precise date, and what is their significance? We may have two clues. First, there are no -ting names in Orkney, that is, names with -ting in the second half of them. The contrast with Shetland is great, and may well suggest that the situation here post-dates the separation of Shetland from the earldom of Orkney in the year 1195. Institutions in Shetland and Orkney which differ often date from the post-separation period.

Figure 7. According to tradition, the Dale ting met on the small promontory called Gulaness.
© *THING Project / Frank Bradford*

Our second clue may lie in two more Shetland -ting names, now obsolete, but recorded in documents of the early 14th century and never again mentioned. In September 1321 the archbishop of Nidaros (Trondheim) presented priests to two parishes in the diocese of Orkney, called *Þvæitaþing* and *Rauðarþing*. According to a related document, written the following year, *Þvæitaþing* was in Shetland, and we can be confident in assuming that *Rauðarþing* was here as well.

I suspect that these names have disappeared without trace not because they are ancient, but because, as Fellows-Jensen suggests, they were modern. I propose that they did not 'catch on', and fell out of use at an early date.

We can now speculate about how Shetland's -ting names came into existence. Given the dates of *Þvæitaþing* and *Rauðarþing*, I propose that we may be looking at a reorganisation like the one that we know was carried out by Duke Håkon Magnusson in Shetland's fiscal affairs. Håkon, no doubt with the assistance of Shetlanders, abolished Shetland's 'Orcadian' land-units and rental and taxation arrangements around 1300, and replaced them with local ones.

What is more likely than that Håkon founded and named our modern parishes as well. I suggest that Shetland's ting-parishes were a result of the 'new broom' that Håkon and his servants were wielding everywhere in Shetland around 1300. It is far less likely that names like Delting and Lunnasting were created later than that. The chaotic period from the Black Death to 1490, when our -ting names begin to appear in documents, is not a time when we should expect major change in the local administration.

My proposal, then, is that Shetland's parish tings date from around 1300: that is, that they post-dated Shetland's connection with the earldom of Orkney, and were contemporary with Shetland's *lawting*. In other words, the establishment of the *lawting*, and of our parishes and their district courts, plus the new assessment of land for rent and tax, were part of the same official programme. King Magnus and King Håkon turned Shetland society upside down.

We have a fairly clear picture, then, of the development of Shetland's *lawting*, and our district tings, from the 1270s until the early 17th century. But what happened before that? After all, Shetland had been a Scandinavian society for more than 400 years when Magnus Lawmender came to the throne. Trying to understand the organisation of justice in Shetland before Magnus's time is a very difficult task. What seems certain is that our ting-arrangements in that distant period were different from, and more complex than, their successors.

Our best information about that distant period may be a document and some place names. In Bergen in September 1490, a division took place of the property of the nobleman Hans Sigurdsson. Hans had lands in Shetland, and the assessors of 1490 listed them along with the rest of his large estate. They must have taken their information from a much older document, because the lands on Shetland's Westside are said to be in *Vogafiordwngh*, and others in the north of Shetland to be in *Mawedes 'otting'* – divisions unknown in any later record.

There is no puzzle about the nature of these Shetland districts: they were quarters and eighths of the islands, old administrative units known in Norway and elsewhere. *Vogafiordwngh* means the 'voes' or Waas quarter; *Mawedes 'otting'*, the eighth at the narrow isthmus, the physical feature – Mavis Grind – that now gives its name to the parish of Northmavine.

Figure 8. Tingaholm and the Gallow Hill.
© THING Project / Frank Bradford

These divisions must have been ancient. They do not resemble any Shetland districts of more recent times. In Norway, quarters and eighths were parts of a whole *fylke* or province, and were early in date. Furthermore, they may have had tings. Norway's Gulating law contains references to quarter-tings, as well as the tings of whole provinces.

Meanwhile, Shetland had a second old division: the *herað*, which appears in several of our place names as 'Herra'. There are Herra-names in Yell, Fetlar, Lunnasting and Tingwall, and they refer to largish districts. Once again the division could have a ting: there is a reference to a '*heraðs þing*' in Magnus Lawmender's code of 1274.

And there were still faint echoes of the idea of a Herra-ting in Shetland 600 years later. In the 1890s the Faroese linguist Jakob Jakobsen visited the island of Fetlar, and '[d]uring my stay ...' he wrote, 'an elderly woman living there told me that, according to an old tradition, the Isle ... was formerly divided into three small districts, each with its own thing, the present "Herra" being one of them.'

The connection made by that woman between the Herra and the law is very striking. But if every little district in Shetland had a ting during that era, the system of justice must have looked very different from the one we know from documents from the late 13th century onwards.

Finally, we must look at Shetland's Gallows Hills. There are more than a dozen of them, in every part of the islands. They are reminders of sites where local rough justice was carried out. Two of them, in the south of Shetland, are called Gulga and Wilga, from Old Norse *gálgi*, meaning gallows. The Gallow Hill in Fetlar lours over the district we have just been discussing called Da Herra. Except in one case, Shetland's Gallow Hills do not bear much relationship to later ting-sites, if any at all, and, once again, we may assume that they are early.

I return to Tingwall, the place in Shetland where we can best ponder over Shetland's tings and their development. A hill called the Hill of Herrislee overlooks the ting valley. The name derives from *herað*, of course. The Herra district here was extensive. As already mentioned, most Gallow Hills in Shetland bore no geographical relation to the later ting-sites. The exception is the Gallow Hill a mile south-west of Tingaholm *(Figure 8)*.

My suggestion is that the holm in the Tingwall Loch had been the site of a *heraðs*-ting, probably a pre-eminent one – maybe even an *althing*, long before the reign of Magnus Lawmender. I propose that it was part of an archaic system of law courts in the islands,

Shetland's territorial and judicial institutions, *before* and *after* 1274

Pre-1274? ...	... and after
Alting?	Lawting
Quarters, eighths – with tings?	-ting-parishes – with tings
Herras – with tings?	Scattalds – without tings

with its gallows nearby, long before a central *lawting* came into existence in the islands. *(Figure 9)*

Shetland might have had an *althing*, a general assembly of free men, during the centuries after the Scandinavian settlement of the islands. If so, it probably met at Tingwall. Sometime in that early period Shetland was divided into administrative units called quarters and eighths, but also into much smaller ones called *héraðs*, which may have had their own tings.

In the late 13th century Magnus Hakonsson's new law code came into use in the islands, and royal officials took control. First the regime established a *lawting* at Tingwall, where the new laws, and revisions to them, were promulgated. But if sheriffs and lawmen were to visit district tings, as we find King Hakon's bailiff doing in the North Isles of Shetland around 1306, there would have been a need to streamline matters. A system of multiple *herað*-tings would have been too burdensome to administer efficiently. It looks as if that is why our new district tings came into existence, at Delting, Sandsting and elsewhere: as part of a reformation by Håkon Magnusson of public life in the islands. The herra-districts, with their tings, were replaced by tax-paying districts called 'scattalds', which had no tings – a more streamlined arrangement.

The new system was long-lived. Three hundred years later Earl Patrick Stewart was still travelling around Shetland's local tings, carried by servants in his sedan chair. He used Magnus Lawmender's code there, and at his *lawting*. It was not until Patrick was removed from the islands, after 1608, that Shetland's tings finally fell into disuse.

Figure 9. Tingaholm and Tingwall Loch.
© THING Project / Frank Bradford

Figure 1. Location map of
Orkney showing places
mentioned in the text.
        © THING Project

Orkney's Things

Sarah Jane Gibbon

The Ting has passed her awfu' doom,
Dat for her fats an' sinfu' deed
Sheu s'ud be taen an' brunt tae ass,
Withoot or mercy, or remeed.[1]

(From *The Play o' de Lathie Odivere,*
by Walter Traill Dennison, published in 1894)

This verse is taken from a ballad based on verses collected in Orkney in the mid 1800s. Set in Norway, it tells the story of a man who swears an oath to Odin in order to marry a beautiful lady and of the relationship between the lonely Lady Odivere and a selkie (a seal who can take the form of a human). Her husband discovers her adultery when he kills her seal child and finds it wearing his chain, and in a rage imprisons her. She is tried, convicted and sentenced to be burnt to death by the thing (who would all have been peers and associates of Lord Odivere), but on the day of execution is saved by the selkie. This combination of fragmentary accounts, legends, folk memories and history to create a ballad with a Norwegian setting, supernatural encounters, oaths, bargaining, trials and justice, is the ideal introduction to Orkney's thing sites *(Figure 1)*.

Orkney's thing sites are rather mysterious. They emerge from the shadows of saga literature, place names and folklore as vestiges of a type of administration of law and justice that has long since been forgotten. And yet they live on through their physical presence in the landscape and the residual sense of these places as different or special, echoing a memory of their importance in the past.

Orkney was under Norwegian rule from the 9th century until 1468, when Orkney's political and ecclesiastical administrations were based on Norwegian principles. Three main sources of evidence elucidate this chapter of our past, namely *Orkneyinga Saga*, archaeology and place names. *Orkneyinga Saga* is a collection of stories based around the earls of Orkney and their exploits, and provides a fascinating insight into Orkney's heroes and villains. Thankfully for the historian, it also provides important information about Orcadian society, particularly from the mid 11th to mid 13th centuries. When combined with fragmentary written sources (contemporary and later), place name and archaeological evidence, it is possible to piece together an impression of Orkney's medieval society, of which things were a significant part.

Orkneyinga Saga portrays a society where things were called when necessary and were mainly consultative assemblies of chief men, but were also for peace negotiations between rival earls, secret meetings of conspirators or war councils. Almost always an earl made the final decision at the thing, though after advice from a group of councillors. The things were held in the most convenient location for the earl and the men involved and were therefore peripatetic, mirroring governance. There was an apparent preference for the things to be held in spring and autumn and, although the locations are not often named, Mainland was the preferred island on which to meet.

Saga compilers only mention things when relevant to the story and so it is possible that regular assemblies were held in the earldom of which we only catch a glimpse in the narrative. In 1016 and 1017 Earl Einar held a spring thing in the east Mainland of Orkney and implied there would be another thing in the spring of 1018. In 1021, Earls Thorfinn and Brusi held a spring thing to decide on the apportionment of the earldom. In spring 1116/1117, Earls Magnus and Hakon proceeded to the 'meeting place of the Thing of the Orkneymen' on Mainland (Taylor 1938, 206). The following spring they met again, this time on Egilsay. In spring 1136, Earl Paul held a thing on Mainland, and Rognvald held a thing in May 1136 in Kirkwall, which lasted three days. In spring 1139, a meeting was held in Caithness (possibly at Thingswa, west of Thurso, ON *Þing-svað*) where the division of the earldom between Earl Rognvald and Earl Harald was agreed. In spring 1151 Earl Rognvald summoned a 'full Thing on the Mainland' attended by 'all the chiefs that were in his realm' (Taylor 1938, 285). In autumn 1152, Earl Erlend summoned a thing in Kirkwall to receive oaths of allegiance. In autumn 1153, a peace meeting was held in Kirkwall, and in May 1155, Rognvald held a peace meeting in St Magnus Cathedral *(Figure 2)*. At no time is the thing given a designation such as *lawting* or *alting*, but the use of the term 'thing' and the actions taken indicate an assembly recognisable as a lawting taking place.

As well as mentioning thing meetings, *Orkneyinga Saga* also tells us a little about those who were responsible for the making of laws in Orkney. In the latter part of Earl Thorfinn Sigurdsson's story (from about 1050), he is credited with turning his mind

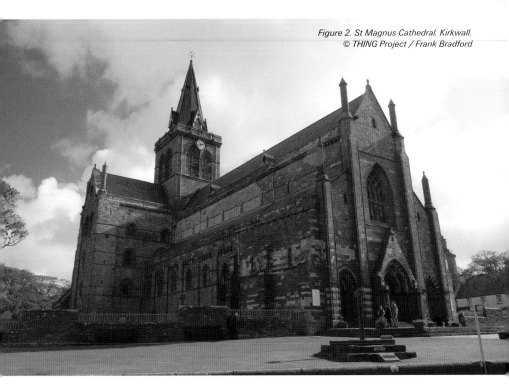

to the government of his land and people and to the making of laws. After receiving absolution for the murder of his cousin Magnus, Earl Hakon Paulsson returned to Orkney and, in the early 12th century, introduced new laws 'which the bonder thought much better than those that were before' (Taylor 1938, 213). In 1137, Earl Rognvald Kolsson held a thing and introduced a law imposing a hereditary claim of land by the earls of Orkney. It is unclear to what extent these accounts of law-making are accurate, but they do tell us that the success of an earl was, at least in part, measured by his ability to govern and issue laws, and that the earl was the dominant lawman in Orkney.

We read in *Orkneyinga Saga* that, by the mid 12th century, meetings tended to be held in Kirkwall, often in St Magnus Cathedral. The cathedral was founded in 1137 and soon afterwards the seat of the bishop of Orkney was transferred here from Birsay. It is highly likely that the seat of the earl was similarly transferred to Kirkwall at this time. As part of this reorganisation of power, parishes were created and a more structured form of secular and ecclesiastical administration imposed. This reorganisation was thorough and successful, and replaced existing administrations. It seems plausible that the judicial system was altered as part of this rearrangement and, as a result, that Kirkwall and St Magnus Cathedral became the main assembly place in Orkney. Local courts continued to be held and, from this time on, parish churches were the preferred venues, with manor houses also being used where appropriate.

Another place in Kirkwall has been suggested as a thing site. This became known by the names 'Parliament House' and 'Parliament Close'and was the court house of the 16th-century Stewart earls of Orkney *(Figure 3)*. This is located in the oldest part of Kirkwall, near the shore and very close to the church of St Olaf, and so it is possible that things were held here in saga times. However, there is no supporting evidence and the area has been much altered since the medieval period.

Certainly, we have evidence from the 15th century that the cathedral was the place of assembly for the most serious trials and disputes. The first record of an assembly in Orkney after the saga period refers to a meeting of good men in the vestry of St Magnus Cathedral some time before 1438. The second is to a *hirdmanstein* meeting, also in the cathedral. The term *hirdmanstein* refers to what originally would have been a meeting of the earl's bodyguard, but by this time was the January meeting of the *lawting*. The use of this term, along with the designations 'lawting' for the week-long June assembly, 'Allhallow Court' for the November assembly and 'Wapenstein' for a February assembly in Kirkwall, may be taken as evidence that things had been held in Orkney from the time of Norwegian rule, and that their Old Norse designations had become corrupted over time and their original meaning altered. In 1573, over a century after Orkney became part of Scotland, Earl Robert Stewart holds the 'harmansteine,'

namely, the Sheriff Court of Orkney in St Magnus Cathedral. In 1611, Orkney was placed under Scottish legal jurisdiction and no longer adhered to its Norse-based law code which was an adaptation of that of the

Figure 3. A plaque marking the site of the court house of the 16th-century Stewart earls of Orkney, Kirkwall.
© THING Project / Frank Bradford

Gulating in Norway. As a result, the already much-altered designations became Scottish and we find no further reference to 'lawtings', although the courts remained unique to Orkney in their composition and role.

So, St Magnus Cathedral in Kirkwall was probably the location of the lawting of Orkney from the later 12th century. The south transept chapel and aisle were known as the 'Court House'. The cathedral contains a bottle dungeon, had a condemned cell in the tower and is the store place of a reputed hangman's ladder and gallows cross-beam *(Figures 4-5)*. The close proximity of the cathedral to the market cross where burnings took place, and its near proximity to 'Gallow Ha', or Heiding Hill, where the gallows and strangling post were located,

Figure 4. Marwick's Hole, the condemned cell in St Magnus Cathedral.
© THING Project / Frank Bradford

indicates that this building was central to the judicial governance of Orkney, as well as the ecclesiastical. Many of Orkney's witch trials were held in the cathedral, and the condemned were confined in Marwick's hole whilst awaiting punishment, before being taken to the top of the hill to be strangled and burnt.

In Kirkwall, then, we have a possible early thing site near the shore and a later thing site in St Magnus Cathedral. But Kirkwall is not the only thing site in Orkney. There is place name evidence for two further thing sites at Tingwall and Dingieshowe, and Maeshowe and the Neolithic monuments at Brodgar have also been suggested as possible thing sites.

Figure 5. The hangman's ladder in St Magnus Cathedral.
© THING Project / Frank Bradford

Figure 6. Tingwall, Orkney.   © THING Project / Frank Bradford

Tingwall (ON *Þing-völlr*, meaning thing-field) in Rendall is first mentioned in *Orkneyinga Saga* as the homestead of Helgi, uncle of the infamous Sweyn Asleifsson *(Figure 6)*. The name applies to the whole settlement area (or township), in which Helgi's farm was the principal dwelling. Townships tend to have topographic names and so the fact this area is named after the thing suggests that the thing was a significant feature when the township was named.

The township of Tingwall is close to the shore on the east coast of west Mainland. It is located on good farmland at a strategic access point for connecting the inner north isles to the Mainland. Centrally placed within the township is the farm and mill of Tingwall, which are adjacent to substantial archaeological remains thought by antiquarians to have been the assembly site. In fact the remains are of an Iron Age broch on which there is evidence of later disturbance and use. No evidence of Norse occupation has been found, but neither have there been any excavations in this vicinity.

Tingwall is close to the boundary between Evie and Rendall, and the two main farms between Tingwall and the boundary are called Midgarth and Midland. This implies that when these farms were named they were in the middle of something. This makes little sense today as they are on the edge of the parish, but if they were named before the parish boundary was there, then they would lie between Tingwall and Woodwick, a large township in Evie parish, thus forming a larger area incorporating the thing site on one side and Vishall (Sacred) Hill on the other. On the slope of Vishall Hill are the farms of Hellicliff (holy path) and Gallowhill (site of gallows), suggesting there was a place of execution on the hill and that the hill was considered sacred or holy. In addition there is a curious legend that associates Tingwall with a hogback burial stone and a high status settlement. The story tells that a hogback stone was erected in the south yard of Tingwall to mark the grave of a queen who had died there, whilst visiting the chamberlain of Orkney. The hogback stone is now lost and the legend forgotten, but the south yard exists and, in the 17th century, the chamberlain of Orkney resided at nearby Woodwick.

The saga reference, place names, archaeological evidence and legend combine to indicate that this place was a settlement area from the Iron Age onwards, that in saga times it was the home of a wealthy man, and that it was associated with justice and execution before the parishes were formed. Tingwall's role as a place of assembly did not continue into the later medieval period, but this does not mean it was not a significant place in the earlier medieval landscape of Orkney.

Dingieshowe (ON elements *þing* and *haugr*, thing-mound) is located on the isthmus that joins the peninsula of Deerness to the Mainland *(Figures 7 and 11)*. The mound comprises the substantial remains of an Iron Age broch, with evidence of occupation since the Neolithic period. Today the mound forms part of a fragile barrier of sand dunes that run the length of the isthmus. Based on its name and location, it is likely to have been where Einar held his thing meetings in 1016 and 1017. Amundi and Thorkel resided close by at Skaill in Deerness and this is the only neutral central location in the area that could have served as a meeting place. The site, like Tingwall, is

Figure 7. Dingieshowe, Orkney.
© THING Project / Frank Bradford

centrally located within a township that straddles the parish boundary, indicating that it was a cohesive unit prior to the division of the parishes. This is further supported by the fact that both Deerness and St Andrews claim Dingieshowe as part of their parish.

As well as the place name Dingieshowe, the nearby district of Toab (ON *toll hóp*, toll bay), may refer to the role of this place as a taxation point for foreign ships. Earl Paul mustered his fleet in Deer Sound in the 12th century, and in the 18th century ships frequently came into Deer Sound to sell produce and recruit men. A Pictish stone at nearby Greens indicates that the area served as a gathering place in the pre-Viking era, and in more recent times, travellers camped on the isthmus and sold their produce there. In short, there are long-standing meeting and mercantile traditions associated with this area, in keeping with its original function as a thing site.

There are many local stories and traditions about Dingieshowe. It has been variously described as the haunt of fairies, a sacred place, and the home of trows (small beings that live in mounds in Orkney and are known to like fiddle music). A local story centred on the mound tells of a fiddle player who is lured into the mound by a trow and, after a night of playing, leaves the mound only to find he has been gone for 14 years. This liminal shore location was considered the home of the devil and all his subjects; it was where selkies gathered and danced, where sea-monsters were witnessed and, being neither land nor sea, belonged to no-one. Another, more sinister story, which tells of a beheaded witch who was buried at the isthmus, but whose head repeatedly reappeared from its burial place, is perhaps indicative of trial and punishment having taken place nearby.

Several other places in the Stenness area have been suggested as possible thing sites. Certainly there is a similar air of mystery and superstition surrounding the great Neolithic complex at the Stenness/Sandwich border in west Mainland *(Figure 8)*. Here again we have

Figure 8. The Ring of Brodgar, looking south-east across Stenness. © *THING Project / Frank Bradford*

evidence of settling disputes and making alliances in a place that was traditionally revered and feared in equal measure. There is telling of an annual feast which took place in the church of Stenness on New Year's Day, when people brought supplies and danced and ate for four to five days before returning home. This was an opportunity for people to meet and young people often exchanged oaths during the festivities. They would go to the temples of the sun and moon (the Ring of Brodgar and the Stones of Stenness), before meeting at the Stone of Odin (a now-destroyed standing stone) and passing their hands through a hole in the stone to seal their engagement to each other – a form of oath deemed sacred. Sick infants and injured people were brought to the stone to be cured and oaths to Odin were sworn there. These curative and contractual functions mark this area out as special and the combination of pre-Christian and Christian traditions illustrate the longevity of the beliefs.

The stone circles are located on an isthmus between the lochs of Stenness and Harray, and are placed liminally and centrally. They lie within the parish of Stenness, but geographically they would fit better within Sandwick parish. It is believed that the isthmus was donated to the church of Stenness by a pious benefactor who received the right to be buried in the church in return. There is a longstanding association of meetings in this area and of contracts being made. In the 16th century several local baillie courts were held in Stenness parish church, so this was also a place of ecclesiastical and secular trial, justice and punishment.

Figure 9. Maeshowe chambered cairn. ` © THING Project / Frank Bradford

Figure 10. One of the many runic inscriptions inside Maeshowe. It is written in two kinds of runes: twigs (top line) followed by plain runic script (below). It translates as: The man who is most skilled in runes west of the ocean carved these runes with the axe which Gaukr Trandilssonar owned in the south of the country (that is, Iceland).
© THING Project / Frank Bradford

The magnificent chambered cairn of Maeshowe lies a short distance from the stone circles and is part of the same Neolithic landscape *(Figure 9)*. According to *Orkneyinga Saga*, this prominent tomb was used as a shelter by Vikings during a snow storm in the 12th century. The interior of the tomb contains the largest collection of runic inscriptions outside Scandinavia, confirming that it was visited by Norse settlers *(Figure 10)*. There is also archaeological evidence of a Viking Age embankment around the tomb, indicating that the Norse felt the need to demarcate this site and separate it from the rest of the surrounding landscape over 3,000 years after the original use of the tomb. Later folkloric associations with Maeshowe tell that it was the home of a 'hogboon' (a fickle ancestral spirit that could bring prosperity or poverty to the farm), and that local people scattered ashes on its surface and left offerings of produce. Interestingly, one of the archaeological indicators of a thing site is evidence of multiple fires, so perhaps the basis of some of these traditions stems back to use of the site in the Viking period.

At present we can only postulate that these places were thing sites in the earlier medieval period, but there is some evidence to support this theory. Stenness and Dingieshowe were considered special or sacred by the later population: Stenness as the scene of betrothals, divorces and alliances, and Dingieshowe as a place associated with trials and witch burial – all redolent of activities at thing sites. The place name, Dingieshowe, strongly suggests a thing site, as does that at Tingwall, which also seems to have been remembered by some as a meeting place. We also have the saga evidence and some court records to support the thing site status of all four places. In short, Tingwall, Dingieshowe, Stenness and Kirkwall can all be considered as probable or definite Viking Age thing sites, either as local things (and in the case of Kirkwall at least, probably a lawting), or as part of a peripatetic judicial administration that was superseded by the centralising reforms of the mid to late 12th century. The success of these reforms means that only small fragments of the earlier systems of secular, ecclesiastical and judicial governance linger in the pages of *Orkneyinga Saga* – in place names, folklore and archaeological discoveries. Yet these fragments provide tantalising glimpses of the beginnings of a form of judicial representation that influenced our islands for almost a millennium.

Endnotes

1   Translated as: *The Ting has passed her awful doom | That for her faults and sinful deed | She should be taken and burnt to ash | Without mercy or remediation.*

Figure 11. Dingieshowe, Orkney.
© THING Project / Frank Bradford

Figure 1. Map of northern Scotland showing the medieval provinces, and the location of Dingwall.
© THING Project

Dingwall – A Northern Scottish Enigma   *David MacDonald*

The very name, Dingwall, indicates that this place – before it entered into written history – had been a significant centre of Norse government in Ross, one of Scotland's northernmost counties *(Figure 1)*. The origin of the place name lies in Old Norse *þing-völlr* (pronounced 'thing-wall'), meaning the field or meeting place of a parliament or law assembly. That assembly had met in the open air somewhere in, or very near to, what would become the town of Dingwall.

Dingwall, as a centre of Norse government and law, has long posed historians and archaeologists an enigma, a huge puzzle. Dingwall lies a considerable distance from the main areas of Norse settlement in northern Scotland, namely, the Northern Isles of Orkney and Shetland, and the Western Isles or Hebrides. By the time Dingwall entered into historical record in 1226, when it was created a royal burgh, the Viking era in Ross had long passed. Dingwall appears nowhere in any Norse saga. More puzzling still is that no archaeological traces of a settled Norse presence have been uncovered in Ross. The story of the thing site of Dingwall is a detective story.

A double case of mistaken identity

In 1899 a local amateur antiquarian, Robert Bain, published his opinion that the location of *þing-völlr* was to be found on the near vertical eastern face of the Gallowhill, a natural hill which overlooks the town from the west. At the time, and throughout the 20th century, that opinion met with acceptance, largely because nothing was known of Dingwall as a thing site beyond a deductive remark made by the poet Robert Southey in 1819. He observed that the name of 'Dingwall, the capital of Ross-shire' reminded him 'of the Icelandic capital Thingvalla'. Thingvalla, better known today as Thingvellir, was from AD 930 the meeting place of Iceland's *althing*. At Thingvellir, to take advantage of natural amplification, pronouncements of the *althing* court were made in front of a rock cliff face. An opinion that the steep face of Gallowhill had served the same purpose at Dingwall seemed not unreasonable *(Figure 2)*.

Figure 2. Looking east across Gallowhill. The precipitate descent of the face of Gallowhill (Gallaber) is marked by the line of tress and hides the town below from view. © THING Project / Frank Bradford

Burgh land records, however, reveal an older name for Gallowhill: Gallaber. This latter place name derives from Old Norse *galgeberg* (hill of the gallows). This revelation casts doubt on the belief that the location of the Norse place of execution had also served as the meeting place of the Dingwall thing court. A medieval site of judicial execution, which had occupied the same location as that of the court, is an extremely rare phenomenon. In practically every case, the execution site had been located some distance removed from the meeting place of the court.

Robert Bain also claimed that the eastern face of Gallaber had later acted as the medieval moothill of Dingwall, the existence of which he understood from a reported document of 1503. Again, that thought appeared to be based on reason. Scottish medieval moothills shared a fundamental characteristic with all thing sites. They were locations of outdoor law courts at which law and justice were enacted and proclaimed. A moothill was always an elevated site of some kind – a small natural hill, a hill slope, or a man-made mound. Some thing sites, but not all, had made use of the same type of feature, but many thing sites simply occupied a level grassy area, as the Norse place name *þing-völlr* implies. *Þing-völlr* sites which did make use of a raised, but low, eminence possessed what was termed in Norse a *løg-berg* (law-hill), or a *þing-haugr* (thing-mound). These acted as a stage to heighten both the visibility and the audibility of the law council. If the *þing-völlr* at Dingwall, or the moothill of Dingwall, had made use of such a feature, that feature was unlikely to have been Gallaber, because courts of assembly practically never met on the site of judicial execution.

The moothill of Dingwall and *þing-völlr*

By the document of 1503 James Duke of Ross resigned all of his lands of Ross, except the moothill mound of Dingwall, which, in 1503, yet retained aura of law sufficient to allow him to keep the title Duke of Ross. The moothill, according to the document, lay right beside the town of Dingwall, not a distance from it. Moothills were often referred to simply as 'Hill', for example, 'Hill of Dingwall' and, in 18th-century land records, a property in Dingwall named as the Yardhill, or Hillyard, is reported as being 'now the burial place of the family of Cromartie'. Today that property is a car park, which at its centre contains a tall monument erected on the top of the Cromartie burial place *(Figure 3)*. This car park, formerly the Hillyard, lies immediately south of the ancient parish churchyard of Dingwall and 600m eastwards of Gallowhill. In the same way that the churchyard encloses the church of Dingwall, the Hillyard had enclosed the Hill of Dingwall.

The 1st Earl of Cromartie's title deed to the Hillyard, dated 1672, confirms the property as 'ye mute hill of Dinguall'. Its location right beside the medieval burgh named Dingwall provides a strong indication that the moothill is the very same mound which had been the *løg-berg*, or *þing-haugr*, of *þing-völlr*.

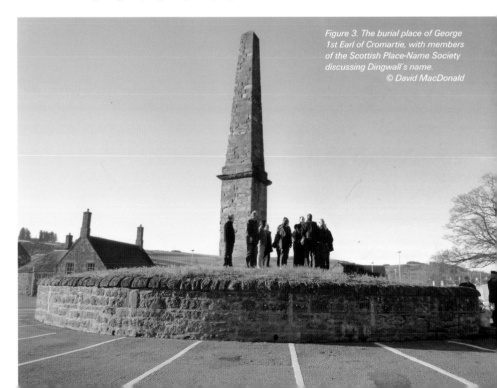

Figure 3. The burial place of George 1st Earl of Cromartie, with members of the Scottish Place-Name Society discussing Dingwall's name.
© David MacDonald

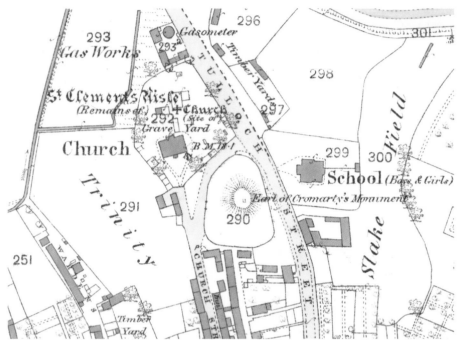

Figure 4. Ordnance Survey map of 1881 illustrating the assembly complex of church, mound and Trinity field.
© *National Library of Scotland*

Cromartie's monument and the mound on which it stood are clearly indicated on the Ordnance Survey map of 1881, and contiguous to the mound is the churchyard *(Figure 4)*. Contiguous to both is the field, or croft, of Trinity. These three features identify an assembly complex of remarkable similarity to that of the Isle of Man. The Manx Tynwald (*þing-völlr*) assembly place similarly comprises a church, the mound of Tynwald Hill and, alongside both, a gathering field. On the three components of the *þing-völlr* of Dingwall, similar activities to those which still take place annually on the Tynwald assembly place would have occurred.

Geophysical survey of the car park in 2011 by Oliver O'Grady may have confirmed this association, although this has yet to be tested through archaeological excavation *(Figure 5)*. The geophysical survey results indicate that the assembly mound, around 40m in diameter, was surrounded by a probable ditch, with a possible ramp and bridge crossing the ditch leading northwest towards the parish church. It is very tempting to see this as the beginnings of a processional way linking the church and the *þing*-mound

Figure 5. Interpretative
diagram of the Dingwall
thing mound and
medieval church based on
geophysical survey.
© Oliver O'Grady

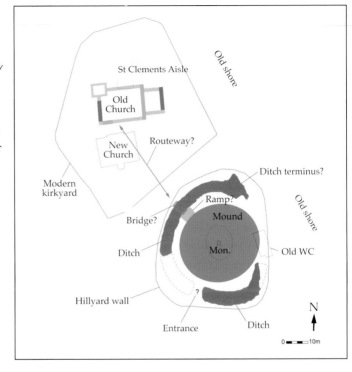

of Dingwall – just as
at Tynwald. Another
entrance crossing
the ditch to the
south or southwest
may indicate access
to the mound from
the adjacent level
area of Trinity
Croft, which is a
good candidate for
the assembly field
indicated by the
name *þing-völlr* –
Dingwall.

Figure 6. Annotated aerial photograph showing proximity of Dingwall to the sea.
© RCAHMS. Licensor RCAHMS / aerial.rcahms.gov.uk

Slaik and historical topography

Tulloch Street (constructed in the 1830s by means of infill) forms the eastern boundary of the Cromartie car park. Across Tulloch Street lay Slakefield. According to the title deed of 1672 the Hillyard had then been bounded at its east by *'the common slaik'*. In 1684 *'Slaick'* formed the northern boundary of the Trinity Croft. In1787 *'slaik'* had lain immediately both northwards and eastwards of the parish churchyard. Indeed in burgh land records of the 17th and 18th centuries, *'slaik'* appears as the northern boundary of many of the burgh land-holdings on the north side of the High Street. These boundaries are described variously as *'the slaik'*, *'the sea'*, *'the floodmark'*, or *'the fludder'* (cf. *fløda*, Shetland Norn, meaning reaching high water). Slaik therefore can be understood as land which the sea had 'licked over' at high water (ON *sleikja*, to lick) *(Figure 6)*.

A plan drawn in 1790 by the surveyor George Brown, on which he represented the sea at Dingwall at high water, shows sea immediately east of both the churchyard and the Hillyard, and sea flowing over what became Slakefield after the completion of the embankments of the Dingwall Canal in 1817 *(Figure 7)*. The name *cruik* (Scots or ON, bend), given to the islets on Brown's plan, indicates that in the past these had been lands contained within bends of the river. Alteration of the course of the river had left them as islets. Clearly, therefore, there had been convenient beaching places for the ships of thing-goers in the immediate vicinity of *þing-völlr*.

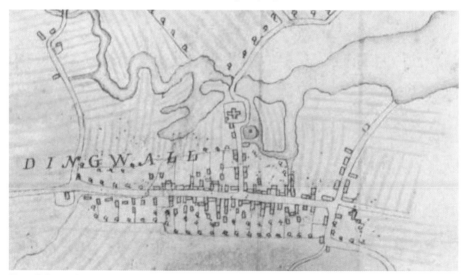

Figure 7. Extract from a 1790 plan of Dingwall drawn by surveyor, George Brown.
© Crown Copyright: National Archives of Scotland (reference number RHP 11591 – 00001)

The Holy Trinity and St Michael

Following the death in 1504 of James Duke of Ross, there is no further record of the moothill until a crown charter in 1591 released all the chaplainry lands of the Holy Trinity and St Michael lying within Dingwall. These included the Trinity Croft and its enclosure, named as the Hillyard, and also a portion of Gallowhill – three components of the assembly complex. Centuries earlier the church of Dingwall had been given to the Priory of Urquhart, founded in Moray around 1135 by King David I as a cell and dependency of the Abbey of Dunfermline, the royal abbey of David's line. Not until the later 15th century did the Abbot of Dunfermline finally approve release of the church of Dingwall to the diocese of Ross. The dedications of both Dunfermline Abbey and Urquhart Priory were to the Holy Trinity. A burgh land record of 1682 tells that the chaplainry lands of St Michael (alias Aikermichael), and presumably those of the Holy Trinity too, had been held of the Abbey of Dunfermline. In sum, all this leads to the deduction that David I had given the assembly complex at Dingwall to the monks of Dunfermline, probably in the hope of 'neutering' it as the co-ordinating centre in Ross of Gaelic-Norse opposition to his advancement of Anglo-French feudalism.

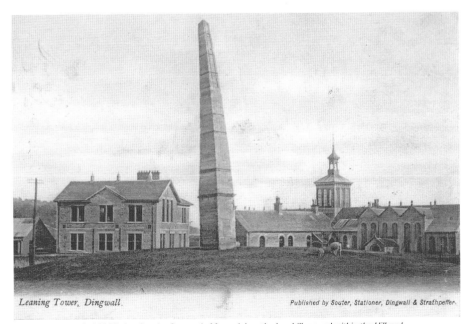

Leaning Tower, Dingwall.   *Published by Souter, Stationer, Dingwall & Strathpeffer.*

Figure 8. Postcard of 1902 showing the Cromartie Memorial on the law-hill mound within the Hillyard.
© Dingwall Museum Trust

David I's birth is dated to AD 1083x1085, only two decades after the death (AD 1060x1065) of Thorfinn the Mighty, Norse ruler of Ross. Since the authority of medieval moothills was dependent on their considerable antiquity, it is highly likely that the identified medieval assembly place at Dingwall is the same assembly place as the *þing-völlr* which gave Dingwall its name. Moreover, the survival until 1226 of the place name *þing-völlr*, Its initial 'th' sound changed by Gaelic usage to the 'd' sound, suggests that Gaelic speaking descendants of a Norse ruling elite in Ross had retained within their spoken Gaelic – at least into the 12th century – the Norse name for their centre of assembly, law and government. How else in the Gaelic speaking environment of Ross could the essentially Norse place name Dingwall have survived to become the name of a Scottish royal burgh in 1226?

Cromartie Memorial Car Park

In 1703, Queen Anne erected Sir George Mackenzie to the title of Earl of Cromartie. In 1707 Lord Ross of Hawkhead petitioned the Queen, asking that he be made Earl of Ross. If Hawkhead's petition was to succeed, Cromartie and all the proud Mackenzie gentlemen of Ross would be classed as socially inferior to the newly created Earl of all Ross. Cromartie, enraged by the very thought of such an outcome, successfully thwarted this potential demeaning of all Mackenzies. In celebration of success he raised a remarkably tall obelisk on the central summit of the moothill of the capital of Ross to symbolise that no man from then on would ever be installed Earl of Ross on that spot *(Figures 8-9)*. On the death of George 1st Earl of Cromartie, in 1714, his mortal remains were interred close to the base of his outrageously tall obelisk.

In 1948 the Cromartie Estate granted the mound to the town of Dingwall to fulfil a need for a town centre car park. In return, the burgh council undertook to retain and maintain the central burial place and the monument, by then an early 20th-century reduced replica of the original.

Celtic Connections

The similarity of the identified *þing-völlr* at Dingwall to the assembly complex of the Manx Tynwald Hill suggests that it was Vikings from the region of the Irish Sea who were the founders of Viking Ross and its *þing* site. The Icelandic saga, *Book of Settlements* (*Landnámabók*), tells that, in the late 9th century, Thorstein the Red, son of Aud, daughter of the Norse ruler of the Hebrides, and of Olaf, first Norse king of Dublin, co-led with Sigurd Earl of Orkney a conquest of northern Scotland. Consequent to Alex Woolf's recent historical locating of the Pictish kingdom of *Fortriu* to Moray and Ross, we

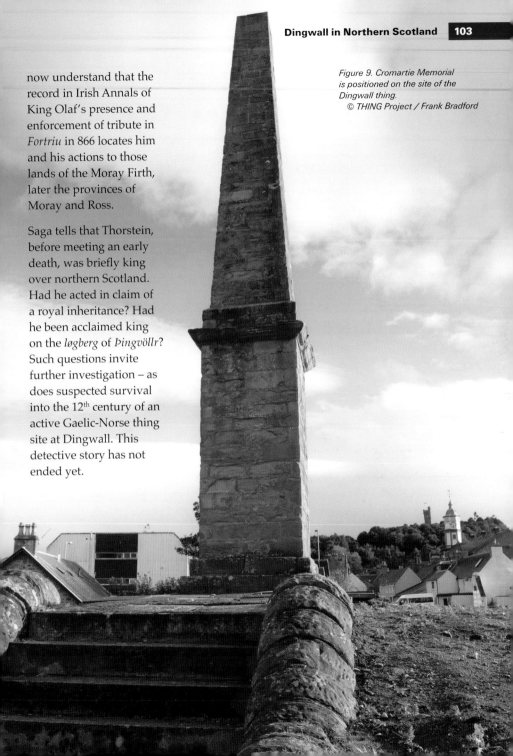

now understand that the record in Irish Annals of King Olaf's presence and enforcement of tribute in *Fortriu* in 866 locates him and his actions to those lands of the Moray Firth, later the provinces of Moray and Ross.

Saga tells that Thorstein, before meeting an early death, was briefly king over northern Scotland. Had he acted in claim of a royal inheritance? Had he been acclaimed king on the *løgberg* of *Þingvöllr*? Such questions invite further investigation – as does suspected survival into the 12th century of an active Gaelic-Norse thing site at Dingwall. This detective story has not ended yet.

Figure 9. Cromartie Memorial is positioned on the site of the Dingwall thing.
© *THING Project / Frank Bradford*

Figure 1. Location
map of the Isle of
Man, showing places
mentioned in the text.
© THING Project

Tynwald – Ancient Site, Modern Institution   *Andrew Johnson*

Introduction

The Isle of Man prides itself in its parliament, Tynwald, both as a place (Tynwald Hill) and an institution (Tynwald Court), and in its claim to be the oldest continuous parliamentary assembly in the world. Today, the Island is governed by the modern iteration of Tynwald, a bicameral parliament that makes its decisions by majority consensus. Thus it is Tynwald Court as an institution that is seen to govern, rather than a party or coalition of one particular political persuasion that may be changed at the next election.

Together with the majority of the machinery of government, Tynwald Court is now based in Douglas, the modern capital. Every 5 July – Old Midsummer's Day – Tynwald returns to its roots, however, and assembles in the open air to hear its new laws promulgated from Tynwald Hill before the people, in a ceremony attended by thousands.

Location

The Isle of Man lies towards the northern end of the Irish Sea, approximately equidistant from Cumbria, Northern Ireland and southwest Scotland (Burrow Head in the Scottish county of Dumfries and Galloway is just 29km from the Point of Ayre, the nearest point on the Isle of Man). Nearly 50km long and 16km wide, the Isle of Man covers an area of about 580 square kilometres, and rises to a high point – Snaefell – of 621m *(Figure 1)*.

Tynwald Hill stands close to the centre of the Isle of Man, in a natural amphitheatre surrounded by several summits rising 300–400m to the east and southwest, some 2-4km away. It is located on a small plateau of sand and gravel between a river to the north and smaller tributary streams to the south. Natural routeways likely to have been in use for centuries lead to the site from the west, north, south and east. An important

Figure 2. An aerial view of Tynwald Hill and the surrounding area in the 1950s. Pagan and Christian burials from a thousand years ago were found in the sand and gravel quarries around the plateau on which Tynwald stands.
© *Manx National Heritage*

natural harbour, the port of Peel, lies 4km to the west and is guarded by fortifications on St Patrick's Isle in the harbour mouth. Peel was the Island's primary link to the rest of the maritime Kingdom of Man and the Isles – now the Scottish Hebrides – created by the Norse in the 11th century AD.

Today, the three principal historical features of the site are Tynwald Hill itself, a four-tiered assembly mound standing just over 3m high, and the Royal Chapel of St John the Baptist, which is connected to the hill by a processional way *(Figure 2)*. The current chapel was built in 1847-9, and all three elements are enclosed within a precinct wall also constructed in 1849. The chapel replaces an older church which itself had developed from an earlier medieval predecessor, and the precinct wall of 1849, which now formalises the area, also replaces an older, less regular earth enclosure around the Hill. Eighteenth-century engravings and maps provide evidence for this, as well as firmly demonstrating that the tiered form of the Hill is at least as old *(Figure 3)*.

Nowadays the site is surrounded by an open fairfield and landscaped arboreta to the north and west, and by the village of St John's to the south and east, for which the chapel was both the attraction and the origin of the modern place name.

Figure 3. A 1787 engraving of Tynwald looking westwards. It shows the steps leading up the Hill, and part of the old enclosure surrounding the Hill (and also surrounding the Chapel of St John, though this cannot be seen).
© Manx National Heritage

Archaeological Context

The modern surroundings and the well-maintained public spaces belie the depth of archaeological evidence which is known from the area.

Tynwald Hill stands close to a substantial Bronze Age burial mound containing a cist which was exposed by road-widening works in 1848 – part of the same Victorian improvements which saw the construction of the present Royal Chapel and the modern enclosure around the Hill. Such burial monuments are generally more than 3,000 years old in the Isle of Man. The road would appear to have truncated the mound in which this cist was set, if the recorded dimensions of 18m by 13m are accurate. It is conceivable that Tynwald Hill was artificially scarped out of a portion of this burial mound, or from another burial mound immediately adjacent. This raises the intriguing possibility that the Vikings may have assumed the burial monuments were near-contemporary rather than prehistoric, and that the place was imbued with a resonance associated with the burial of their own forebears.

Certainly there were several burials of various dates in the area, as reported by Barnwell in 1868:

> In a field near the Tynwald Mount were three kistvaens, one of which was laid bare by a cutting through the road. Near it were the two other similar graves, close to one another, one of which contained a battle-axe and spur, the other a collection of beads and other ornaments and an urn.

The first grave is the Bronze Age burial already described. The other two, one of which another antiquary (Oswald in 1860) describes as 'much smaller in size', are probably medieval 'lintel graves', and lay less than 50m from the Hill. At a later date the hilt and upper blade of a Viking sword was also found less than 100m southwest of the Hill. These are clear evidence of Viking Age graves containing accompanied burials. The finds were removed for examination to a London museum and have long since disappeared.

The demolition of the old chapel at St John's in the 1840s revealed a carved stone cross fragment which bore distinctive 10th-century ring-chain interlace and part of a runic inscription in Old Norse stating: '... but Osruth raised these runes'. There are several instances of lintel graves being found individually to the north of the Royal Chapel, north of the processional way, and also 150m to the south of the Chapel, where more than 30 lintel graves were uncovered in 1937. One of the latter graves was associated with the remains of Viking weapons, including a sword, a spearhead and a shield boss. Reassessment of cemetery evidence on the Isle of Man suggests that pagan Viking settlers were very quickly assimilated into the indigenous Christian community, giving rise to isolated pagan burials, pagan burials within Christian cemeteries, and the raising of stone crosses bearing pagan iconography within a short timeframe of no more than 30 or 40 years.

Further afield there are several other archaeological sites dating to the 1st millennium AD, which together suggest that the wider area around Tynwald Hill was not only an important burial site dating back to prehistoric times, but also one of significant status. Intriguingly, these together imply that Tynwald may have pre-Viking origins, a theory which will benefit from further investigation. No excavation of Tynwald Hill itself has taken place and therefore the date of origin and nature of origin of the site is untested – as is the assumption that the first use of what we now know as Tynwald Hill dates as early (or indeed, as late) as the 10th century AD.

Earliest References to Tynwald

The earliest references to the place name Tynwald appear in the Chronicles of the Kings of Man and the Isles in the Latin forms *tyngualla* and *tingualla* in entries for the years 1228 and 1237, though only the latter was an occasion for a formal assembly *(Figure 4)*. An even earlier Chronicle entry for 1097 records an assembly of chieftains on the Isle of Lewis. This was summoned for the specific purpose of installing a king, and demonstrates that one of the purposes of such assemblies was to legitimise the aspirations of potential royal candidates, and also that assemblies could take place at locations other than Tynwald Hill.

Figure 4. The Chronicles of the Kings of Man from 1228 record King Olaf coming to the place called Tyngualla.
© *THING Project / Frank Bradford*

From the early 1400s, English suzerainty resulted in a written collection of Manx laws; these are now gathered together and known as the Manx Statutes (edited and published by J F Gill in 1883). The Statutes incidentally record the dates and locations of assemblies and the form of such gatherings, and show that the earliest recorded meetings in this period took place at a small number of different locations on the Island, of which Tynwald Hill and Castle Rushen (in the south of the Island) are most often mentioned, along with sites contemporarily named the 'Hill of Reneurling' and 'Killabane': the location of both are known, but no historical features have been identified *(Figure 5)*. The Statutes make clear that Tynwald was – and indeed is – both an assembly and a court. Although the Statutes would seem to imply that a variety of issues needed to be dealt with, the inference is that laws and decisions were recorded only when necessary. Routine matters go unrecorded, whereas laws were written down when there was a need to reaffirm or strengthen them.

It is clear that in the eras of both Norse and English rule disputes were not always easily resolved, and that the concept of peaceful resolution did not always translate into reality. Both of the Chronicle entries for 1228 and 1237 record gatherings that resulted in violence, presumably attracting the chronicler's attention to them, whilst the Statutes

Figure 5. Site commemorating the Killabane assembly, recorded as meeting in this area in 1428.

© THING Project / Frank Bradford

in 1417 and 1422 record risings against the king's lieutenant during sittings of the court. Perhaps indicating that the Manx response to their new English rulers was not entirely positive, the Statutes in 1422 record no less than ten forms of treason, three of which relate specifically to violence and disruption of a Tynwald:

'17. And whosoever constrayneth the Lieutennant by any Means to hould a Tinwald, or any manner of Thing els by Constraint, he breaks the King's Royalty, and that is high Treason.

18. Alsoe whosoever constrayneth the Lieutennant to put down the Lord's Customes or his Prerogatives at the Tinwald, he is a Traytor for the Constraint making by our Law.

19. And whosoever comes with Force and Arms against the Lieutennant's Commandments, especially to the Tynwald, where they should have Right and Reason peaceably, and makes murmur and rising in his Presence, he is a Traytor by our Law.'

The sentence passed upon the traitors of 1422 was execution – that they 'be drawne with wild Horses, hanged, and after that their Heads to be cut off'.

The Tynwald Site Past and Present

The environs of Tynwald Hill have undergone significant change within the last 200 years with the growth of the village of St John's and modernisation of the adjacent roads; part of the periphery of the wider plateau on which it stands has also been quarried away for sand and gravel. Nevertheless, the assembly site still reflects the earliest extant description from the 15th century. This records how the King presided over the assembly facing east, with noblemen, churchmen, officers of the court and the ordinary people gathered around in a defined space according to their status and role within the proceedings. Significantly, this arrangement is described in the 15th century as being the 'Constitution of old Time', implying that it is a well-established practice.

A late 18th-century plan suggests that Tynwald Hill was surrounded by a sub-rectangular enclosure comprising a bank and ditch, which may date back to early post-medieval times and perhaps earlier. Irregularities in its form as shown on this plan suggest that the enclosure around the Hill was enlarged to include the chapel to the east, which had itself been replaced at the close of the 17th century. The enclosure was remodelled to something like its present form in the early 19th century, and the chapel was again replaced when the ceremonial area was modernised between 1847 and 1849 *(Figures 6 and 7)*. This modernisation involved the construction of the new chapel, road

Figure 6. Tynwald Hill today.　　　　　　　　　　© *THING Project / Frank Bradford*

improvements, superficial changes to the appearance of the enclosure which defines the precinct containing the Hill and the Royal Chapel, and a new processional way connecting the two.

The Historical Tynwald Ceremony

The Manx Statutes for 1417–18 detail with considerable precision how the King of Man was expected to preside over Tynwald from the summit of the hill, surrounded by his lords, officers and the common people who were gathered around according to their significance.

Amongst them were 'the worthiest Men in your Land, to be called in, before your Deemsters, if you will ask any Thing of them': these men, comprising a jury of 24, and two judges were at the heart of Tynwald's role as a court. The deemsters were responsible for one's 'doom', or judgement.

These 'worthiest men' are also referred to in the Statutes (using Roman numerals) as the 'xxiiij of the Land', as 'Keys', and as 'Taxiaxi'. The origin, meaning and derivation of the latter two terms is a vexed issue, but 'Keys' has endured as the collective name for members of the lower chamber of Tynwald Court down to the present day.

The deemsters were repositories of common law: this was later described as 'breast law' and directly parallels the role of the Icelandic Lawspeaker, who was expected to know the law by heart. It is clear that this was considered unsatisfactory by the 15th-century English overlords who specifically required in 1422 that difficult points of law be written down as a way of establishing legal precedents. At the time, it was recorded that laws were not customarily recorded, and that this had been the case 'since King Orryes Days'; unfortunately the Statutes are nowhere more specific about which King Godred this might have been! Interestingly, breast law was not done away with until 1636, when again the English administration insisted that it was written down for greater precision.

The Statutes also tell how the assembly was brought to order by one of its officers, the Chief Coroner, who 'fenced' the court, 'that noe Man make any Disturbance or Stirr in the Time of Tinwald, or any Murmur or Rising in the King's Presence, upon Paine of Hanging and Drawing.' This refers to the peaceful principles of assembly that had been in place since Viking times, and dissent from these principles was deemed treason as recorded in 1422. The concept of an enclosure within which disputes could be peacefully resolved is given further historical continuity by the description in the

THE TYNWALD COURT, ISLE OF MAN: THE READING OF THE NEW ACTS.

Figure 7. A contemporary engraving from 1857 showing the promulgation of the new laws from the Hill.
© Manx National Heritage

Chronicles where, in 1237, 'at the assembly itself, after much abuse and vilification against each other, and as no reconciliation seemed possible, the two factions leapt out of the meeting and attacked each other with hostile intent', and by the known existence of various forms of precinct down to the present day.

An essential part of the proceedings as recorded in 1417–18 is a requirement for all present to swear allegiance to the king. In this respect the lords and officers, for all that they sit on the Hill, are no more important than the common people. Otherwise the proceedings were about governance of the Island and the settlement of disputes, and all of this was done according to the laws of the land as interpreted by the deemsters and the Keys.

Figure 8. Each year on the 5th of July, thousands of people gather at Tynwald Hill for the open air meeting of the Tynwald Court (2012).   *© THING Project / Frank Bradford*

Figure 9. The modern Tynwald Court
meets in the island's capital Douglas.
© THING Project / Frank Bradford

The Modern Ceremony and Institution

Today Tynwald Court still formally gathers once a year on Tynwald Hill before a popular audience of thousands *(Figure 8)*. A representative of the British monarch, usually the lieutenant governor, presides over the ceremony, whilst parliament, officials and honoured guests are gathered on, or close to, the Hill. The main business of the public assembly is to hear the titles of new laws created during the preceding year promulgated before the people in Manx Gaelic and English, and to offer the opportunity for personal grievances to be presented in the expectation that some resolution may be achieved *(Figure 10)*.

In these respects, Tynwald continues to perform its ancient duties as a court, though since 1867 its jurors, who are now considered politicians and are referred to as Members of the House of Keys, have been elected to regional constituencies by popular vote, and today form the lower house of Tynwald Court *(Figure 9)*. The lords and officers, who historically sat on the Hill in the early 1400s as the king's council, were gradually replaced by appointees of the king and later the Lord of Man, and today are represented by the upper chamber of Tynwald Court – the Legislative Council – the majority of whose 11 members are chosen by the Keys. Their role is largely to review legislation.

The House of Keys and Legislative Council sit separately and then together as Tynwald Court once a month. The conduct of their business follows procedures common to committees and parliaments the world over, but the combined sitting of the chambers as Tynwald enshrines the collective responsibility that has been a hallmark of this assembly since it began a thousand or more years ago.

Figure 10. Deemsters (judges) lead the procession.   © THING Project / Frank Bradford

Glossary

Althing, allthing, allting, alting, alþing	A general assembly where 'all free men fit to bear arms' had the right to assemble and participate in the procedures. Different spellings relate to different areas and countries
Bailie courts	Courts in each parish or island in Orkney with powers delegated by the earl. They dealt with petty crime and administered matters at parish level. The bailie (judge) was chosen by the leading landowners
Broch	An Iron Age circular stone-built tower with a slight outer batter. Generally about 10m in internal diameter, with walls c 5m thick containing mural chambers, and standing up to 10m high. Found mainly in northern and western Scotland
Doomster, Dempster	The legal officer who pronounced sentence ('doom') at Scottish medieval and later courts
Feudalism	A system of social organisation prevalent in western Europe in medieval times, in which powerful land-owning lords granted privileges and protection to lesser subjects holding a range of positions within a rigid social hierarchy
Goðar (singular *goði*)	Representatives at the Icelandic *althing* or the Faroese *løgting*; *goðorð* means to become a representative or *goði*
hird (ON *hirð*)	Royal or aristocratic retinue or bodyguard
Hirdmanstein	Originally ON *hirðmannstefna*, a meeting of the earl's bodyguard, held in January
Hogback	Massive house-shaped tombstone, typically with curving roof ridge and shingles. Invented in 10th-century York and spread to areas in northern Britain with a Norse presence
Fylki	A grouping of district or communal things in western Norway from which were drawn representatives to the lawthings. Thus, the Gulating law region had six *fylki* which originally sent some 400 representative landowners to the annual thing at Sognefjord. By the 11th century, the representatives were nominated by royal agents who also attended the annual thing, together with numerous clergy chosen by the bishop

Herað	Originally a settled district, which could be quite small and usually had well-defined natural boundaries. Most, if not all, *heraðs* would have had their own things. Later, the same word was used to mean local assembly districts in southeast Norway and adjacent Swedish provinces
Holm	Island
Hundred	This word began to be used widely in Europe for administrative districts from the 9th century. First appears in Sweden on an 11th-century runestone
Kirk	Church
Lawman (ON *løgmaðr*)	In medieval times, the lawman was the judge at provincial and regional things, representing the king as the highest judge in the realm
Lawspeaker	An Icelandic term meaning a man with particular knowledge of the laws, who memorised and mediated the laws when the thing assembled (before the laws were written down)
Lawthing, lawting, *løgting, lagting*	A superior regional assembly, where the regional representatives met (see also *Fylki* above)
Leidang (ON *leiðangr*)	A system imposed on coastal districts in western and southern Norway for the provision and manning of a longship; a military or naval levy
Lintel grave	A grave lined with stone slabs; the usual form of burial on the Isle of Man from early Christian until medieval times (often called 'long cists' in Scotland)
Moot / moothill	Medieval outdoor law courts where law and justice were enacted and proclaimed. A moothill was always elevated – a small hill, hill slope or man-made mound. The 'moot' was the meeting
Picts / Pictish	The name of a Late Iron Age / early historic people in northern and eastern Scotland, famous for their distinctive symbol stones
Þing-haugr	Thing-mound
Þingmenn (singular *þingmaður*)	The men attending the thing
Þing-völlr	Literally 'thing-field'. The field or meeting place of a

	parliament or law assembly
Skeppslag (ship-laws)	Divisions of coastal regions in Norway and Sweden reflecting their obligation to provide ships for military expeditions
Syssel	An administrative district, established first in Jutland before the 11th century. The *syssel* were later replaced by a new type of administrative district in Denmark, the *herred* (plural *herreder*)
Sysselman (ON *sýslumaðr*)	The king's local or regional representative in fiscal, legal, administrative and military matters within a fixed district. Comparable to the English sheriff
Thing, ting, *þing*	Assembly, meeting or parliament
Thingstead, tingstead	Thing place – the place where the thing met
Vápnatak or *þingtak*	The rattling or raising of weapons in the air by the people at the thing assembly to signify their consent
Wapenstein	An assembly held following the *hirðmannstefna* in February (originally ON *vapnastefna*)

Some suggested further reading

Barnwell, P S and Mostert, M (eds), 2003, *Political assemblies in the earlier Middle Ages*. Studies in the Early Middle Ages 7, Turnhout.

Brink, S, 2002, 'Law and legal customs in Viking Age Scandinavia', in Jesch, J (ed), *The Scandinavians from the Vendel period to the tenth century: an ethnographic perspective*, 87-128. The Boydell Press, Woodbridge.

Brink, S, 2004, 'Legal assembly sites in early Scandinavia', in Pantos, A and Semple, S (eds), *Assembly places and practices in medieval Europe*, 205-216.

Brink, S, 2008 (reprinted 2012), 'Law and society: polities and legal customs in Viking Age Scandinavia', in Brink, S and Price, N (eds), *The Viking World*. 23-31. Routledge, Abingdon.

Brink, S and Price, N (eds), 2008 (reprinted 2012), *The Viking World*. Routledge, Abingdon.

Byock, J, 2002, 'The Icelandic althing: dawn of parliamentary democracy', in Fladmark, J M, *Heritage and identity: shaping the nations of the north*, 1-18. The Heyerdahl Institute and Robert Gordon University, Shaftesbury.

Forte, A, Oram, R and Pedersen, F, 2005, *Viking Empires*. Cambridge University Press, Cambridge.

Crawford, B E (ed), 2002, *Papa Stour and 1299*. The Shetland Times, Lerwick.

Darvill, T, 2004, 'Tynwald Hill and the 'things' of power', in Pantos, A and Semple, S (eds), *Assembly places and practices in medieval Europe*, 217-232.

Driscoll, S T, 2004, 'The archaeological context of assembly in early medieval Scotland – Scone and its comparanda', in Pantos, A and Semple, S (eds), *Assembly places and practices in medieval Europe*, 73-94.

FitzPatrick, E, 2004, 'Royal inauguration mounds in medieval Ireland: antique landscape and tradition', in Pantos, A and Semple, S (eds), *Assembly places and practices in medieval Europe*, 44-72.

Graham-Campbell, J (ed), 1994, *Cultural atlas of the Viking world*. Andromeda, Oxford.

Helle, K, 2001, *Gulating og Gulatingslova*. Skald, Leikanger.

Helle, K, 2002, 'Thorvald Thoresson and the political and administrative circumstances in Norway in 1299', in Crawford, B E (ed), *Papa Stour and 1299*, 45-58.

Imsen, S, 2002, 'Tingwall and local community power in Shetland during the reign of Håkon Magnusson, Duke and King', in Crawford, B E (ed), *Papa Stour and 1299*, 59-80.

Ingvaldsen, S, 2012, *Gulatinget*. Selja Forlag, Førde.

Larson, L M, 1935 (reprinted 2008), *The Earliest Norwegian Laws*. University of Illinois, Columbia University Press (reprinted 2008).

Ólafsson, G, 1987, 'Þingnes by Elliðavatn: the first local assembly in Iceland?', in Knirk J (ed) *Proceedings of the tenth Viking Congress, Larkollen, Norway*. Universitetets Oldakssamlings skrifter, ny rekke 9, Oslo.

Owen, O and Driscoll, S, 2011, 'Norse influence at Govan on the Firth of Clyde, Scotland', in Sigmundsson, S (ed), *Viking settlements and society*, 333-46. Hid Íslenzka Fornleifafélag and University of Iceland Press, Reykjavík.

Pantos, A and Semple, S (eds), 2004, *Assembly places and practices in medieval Europe*. Four Courts Press, Dublin.

Roesdahl, E, 1998, *The Vikings* (revised edition). Penguin Books, London.

Roesdahl, E, 2011, 'Scandinavia in the melting-pot, 950-1000', in Sigmundsson, S (ed), *Viking settlements and society*, 347-74. Hid Íslenzka Fornleifafélag and University of Iceland Press, Reykjavík.

Sanmark, A, 2009, 'Administrative organisation and state formation: a case study of assembly sites in Södermanland, Sweden', *Medieval Archaeology* 53, 205-41.

Sanmark, A, 2010, 'The case of the Greenlandic Assembly sites', in *Journal of the North Atlantic*, special vol 2 (2009-10), 178-92.

Sanmark, A and Semple, S J, 2010, 'The topography of outdoor assembly sites in Europe with reference to recent field results from Sweden', in Lewis, H and Semple, S J *Perspectives in Landscape Archaeology*, 107-119. British Archaeological Reports (BAR International Series 2103), Oxford.

Sawyer, B and Sawyer, P, 1993, *Medieval Scandinavia: from conversion to Reformation circa 800–1500*. The Nordic series, vol 17: University of Minnesota Press, Minneapolis and London.

Sawyer, P, 1998, (reprinted) *Kings and Vikings: Scandinavia and Europe AD 700-1100*. Methuen, London.

Skre, D (ed), 2007, *Kaupang in Skiringssal*. Aarhus University Press: Kaupang Excavation Project Publication Series, Vol 1, Norske Oldfunn XXII.

Thorsteinsson, A, 1986, *Tinganes, Tórshavn: en kort historisk orientering (a brief historical guide)*. Føroya Landsstýri, Tórshavn.

Wilson, D M, 2008, *The Vikings in the Isle of Man*. Aarhus University Press, Aarhus.

Þorsteinsson B, 1987, *Thingvellir, Iceland's national shrine: a visitor's companion*. Örn og Örlygur, Reykjavík.

Selected Icelandic sagas and other sources

Broderick, G (ed), 1996, *Cronica Regum Manniae et Insularum (The Chronicles of the Kings of Man and the Isles,* transcribed and translated with an introduction). British Library Cotton Julius A vii.

Dennis, A, Foote, P and Perkins, R (trans), 1980, *Laws of early Iceland: Grágás, the Codex Regius of Grágás, with material from other manuscripts.* Winnipeg, Canada.

Ekrem, I and Mortensen, L B (eds), Fisher, P (trans), 2003, *Historia Norwegiae.* Copenhagen.

Hødnebø, F and Magerøy, H (eds), 1979, *Snorre Sturluson: Norges kongesagaer* (includes *Heimskringla, Ólafs saga ins Helga (Saint Olaf's Saga)).* Den Norske Bokklubben, Oslo.

Karlsson, G, Sveinsson, K and Árnason, M, 1992, *Grágás: mál og menning.* Reykjavík.

Magnusson, M and Pálsson, H (trans), 1979, *Njal's saga* (reprint of 1960). Penguin Books, Harmondsworth.

Pálsson, H and Edwards, P (trans), 1976, *Egil's saga.* Penguin Books, Harmondsworth.

Robberstad, K, 1981, *Gulatingslovi* (4th edition). Det Norske Samlaget, Oslo.

Taylor, A B (trans, intro and notes), 1938, *Orkneyinga saga.* Edinburgh.

Vigfusson, G (ed), 1887, *Icelandic sagas, and other historical documents relating to the settlements and descents of the northmen on the British Isles.* London.

Þorgilsson, A (trans), 1987, *Íslendingabók: Landnámabók.* Jakob Benediktsson, Reykjavík.

Unpublished sources

Nordtveit, E, 2011, *The Gulating Code: origin, character and impact* (unpublished lecture presented at the Thing Project 4th Partner Meeting, 5- 7 April 2011 in Gulen).

O'Grady, O J T, 2008, *The setting and practice of open-air judicial assemblies in medieval Scotland: a multidisciplinary study.* PhD thesis, University of Glasgow.

THING Project partners

Sogn og Fjordane County, Norway (lead partner)
- postmottak.sentraladm@sfj.no
- www.sfj.no

Gulen Municipality, Norway
- postmottak@gulen.kommune.no
- gulatinget@gulen.kommune.no
- www.gulatinget.no

Thingvellir National Park, Iceland
- thingvellir@thingvellir.is
- www.thingvellir.is

Kunningarstovan, Faroe Islands
- torsinfo@torshavn.fo
- www.visittorshavn.fo

Shetland Amenity Trust, Shetland, Scotland
- info@shetlandamenity.org
- www.shetlandamenity.org

Orkney College UHI, Orkney, Scotland
- orkney.college@orkney.uhi.ac.uk
- www.orkney.uhi.ac.uk

Highland Council, Dingwall and Seaforth Ward, Scotland
- dmacdon42@aol.com (Dingwall History Society)
- www.highland.gov.uk

Manx National Heritage, Isle of Man (associate partner)
- enquiries@mnh.gov.im
- www.manxnationalheritage.im